OUR
HEARTS
STILL SING

Also by Peter Millar

Finding Hope Again: Journeying Through Sorrow & Beyond
Waymarks: Signposts to Discovering God's Presence in the World
An Iona Prayer Book
Iona: Pilgrim Guide
(All published by Canterbury Press)

OUR HEARTS STILL SING

Peter Millar

WILD GOOSE PUBLICATIONS

First published 2004 by
Wild Goose Publications, 4th Floor, Savoy House, 140 Sauchiehall St,
Glasgow G2 3DH, UK.

Wild Goose Publications is the publishing division of the Iona Community.
Scottish Charity No. SCO03794. Limited Company Reg. No. SCO96243.
www.ionabooks.com

ISBN 1-901557-86-3   978-1-901557-86-2

Cover illustration 'My Heart Took Flight' © Laura Reiter
www.laurareiter.com

The publishers gratefully acknowledge the support of the Drummond Trust,
3 Pitt Terrace, Stirling FK8 2EY in producing this book.

Overseas distribution:
USA: Just Faith Ministries, Books & Videos, P.O. 221707, Louisville, KY 40252.
Phone: 502.327.3866
Canada: Novalis/Bayard 10 Lower Spadina Ave., Suite 400, Toronto,
Ontario M5E 2Z2
Australia: Willow Connection Pty Ltd, Unit 4A, 3-9 Kenneth Road,
Manly Vale, NSW 2093
New Zealand: Pleroma, Higginson Street, Otane 4170, Central Hawkes Bay

CONTENTS

INTRODUCTION

I first met Peter Millar on the Isle of Iona, where we were members of the
Iona Community's resident group. Peter was the warden of the Abbey,
and I worked alongside his wife, Dorothy, in the Iona Community's shop.
Dorothy managed the shop and purchased the gifts and crafts; I was the
assistant manager and bought the books and music. We were a good
team, and had a succession of wonderful, committed volunteers to help us
throughout the season. Living in community was a privilege and an amazing experience. It wasn't easy though. It could be demanding and stressful.
There were a hundred and fifty new guests to welcome at the centres each
week, hundreds of pilgrims visiting the island, thousands of tourists. On
top of my work in the shop, I had community chores; worship to prepare
(never a chore); resident group meetings, family group meetings and All
Staff meetings to attend; ceilidhs and discos in the village hall to help run
… Being a member of the resident group was 'life in all its fullness'; you
needed to be rooted.

Peter would often pop into the shop to talk to Dorothy and say hallo to
the shop team. I looked forward to his visits. Peter was always inspired or
moved by something – a letter he'd received, an article in a newspaper, a
quote from a book, a conversation he'd shared with a guest or a pilgrim on
the road, the heady scent of the Abbey herb garden, the pulse of the
sunlight on the sea … He came into the shop and brought me out of
myself, back into the wider world. Peter had an energy. He'd sort of dance-
walk in with the life force flowing through him. He was alive, and I was
immediately drawn to him. He was a man of deep feeling and rich experience – he'd lived and worked in South India, West Africa, the East end of
Glasgow. We'd have little talks in the office of the shop, which was off the

Abbey cloisters at that time. He was an open person you could share your thoughts and feelings with, your dreams and confusions. We talked about a great range of things, about a lot of the subjects in this book – prayer and politics, work and worship, the possibility and potential of the now – and soon became friends. In the words of an African saying, we 'laughed together and cried together'; sometimes we shared very bad jokes (Peter's mostly). Peter was a kindred spirit and became a soul friend.

He said a lot of things that stuck with me, that stay with me still now, more than five years later:

I remember, one tangled, difficult day, Peter saying that it was all right that I didn't understand myself; he didn't understand himself either. (It was refreshing to hear that confession from a church minister.)

'You don't understand yourself, I don't understand myself. All of us – we're full of contradictions and confusions. It's human,' he said. 'But God loves us anyway. And Jesus understands.'

That made me feel much better. Knowing that I was understood by Jesus helped me to be gentler with myself; feeling loved and held by God helped me to reach out and to embrace life.

Peter taught me a lot about learning 'to live more calmly within the confusions of my spirit'. He'd learned this himself over many years. Peter helped me to accept myself. And he did this very gently and humanly.

When I think of Peter and his writing, that is the first word that comes to me – 'human'. Peter is one of the most human people I know – loving, affirming and enabling; fragile, vulnerable, sensitive and broken in places; profoundly interested in people and in the human condition; ever open to 'meeting Christ in the stranger'.

The other word that comes to me when I think of Peter and his writing is 'passion' – passion for life, passion for justice. Peter's prophetic and poetic sermons fed and fired and challenged me when he preached in the

Abbey on Sunday mornings.

Before I came to Iona I believed that Christianity was passionless and unconnected to the real world; that Christians were unengaged and judgemental, sin-obsessed and life-denying – anti-women, anti-gay, anti-nature … But on Iona I found something different, something that I always suspected: that Jesus Christ came, rather, to bring Life, life in all its fullness – to bring good news to the poor, to heal the blind, to free the oppressed, the exploited, the marginalised. I identified with the Iona Community's justice and peace commitment, and began exploring its discipline of meditation and action, prayer and politics; it wasn't long before I experienced a feeling of everything falling strangely and unexpectedly into place.

Peter Millar brought me close to Jesus Christ, which is ironic because I don't think he believes in trying to convert people at all. He seems much more interested in listening to people, in sitting alongside folk and learning from them – there is a lesson in 'mission' to be grasped here. I wasn't converted to Christianity by bible bashing or with fear, but by gentle people like Peter who tried to live the gospel in a modern way, and who helped me to recognise 'the larger Christ'; people working to build God's Kingdom on earth and to save lives now; people who confessed their own contradictions and shortcomings, but who tried their best to affirm and enable others.

The times Peter and I spent together each day were moments that left me more rooted and ready to serve. Peter is a great believer in the power and potential of moments. I hope that these short readings, these moments, leave you more rooted and ready to serve.

NEIL PAYNTER
Easter 2004

Lord of every pilgrim heart,
bless our journeys
on these roads
we never planned to take,
but
through your
surprising wisdom
discovered
we
were
on ...

PETER MILLAR

in memory of Dorothy,
soul-mate and inspirational global person

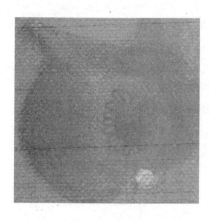

EACH MOMENT CONTAINS
A SACRAMENTAL POSSIBILITY

To become aware of the sacramental nature of the cosmos,
to be open to the sacramental possibilities of each moment,
to see the face of Christ in every person:
these things are not novel,
but their rediscovery
is the beginning of our health.

RON FERGUSON,
a former leader of the Iona Community

In my own journey it took many years before my soul grasped the fact that the cosmos is sacramental, and that each moment in time contains a sacramental possibility. If I had been born into an indigenous culture this soul-knowledge would have been a part of me since childhood.

As I grow older these particular insights take on a new depth of meaning. This is not merely an intellectual understanding; it is within our souls that we make this rediscovery. It is a conversion: We see things freshly – sometimes as if for the first time. Behind all of reality we sense the mystery of 'God's abiding' (as we say in Scotland).

I have always valued these words by the medieval mystic Meister Eckhart:

> *Apprehend God in all things,*
> *for God is in all things.*
>
> *Every single creature is full of God*
> *and is a book about God.*
> *Every creature is a word of God.*
>
> *If I spent enough time with the tiniest creature –*
> *even a caterpillar –*
> *I would never have to prepare a sermon.*
> *So full of God*
> *is every creature.*

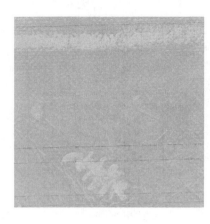

EVERYONE CARRIES THE DIVINE IMAGE

'How can we determine the hour when the night ends and the day begins?' asked the teacher.

'When from a distance you can distinguish between a dog and a sheep?' suggested one of the students.

'No,' was the answer.

'Is it when one can distinguish between a fig tree and a grapevine?' asked a second student.

'No.'

'Please tell us the answer then.'

'It is,' said the wise teacher, 'when you can look in the face of a human being and you have enough light to recognise in her or him your brother or sister. Up till then it is night and darkness is still with us.'

TALES OF THE HASIDIM

In this Hasidic tale lies a great truth. Our society is in darkness if we fail to recognise each other as sister or brother. Our task is to return constantly in our imagination to the fact that everyone carries the divine image. Without that conviction, we become isolated individuals, often carrying within our lives a heavy baggage of prejudice and intolerance. It is paradoxical that the forces of globalisation have made us, in this respect, more distant from one another.

In one of his prayers, the late biblical scholar William Barclay wrote:

> *O God, help us to remember*
> *that you have your own secret stairway*
> *into every heart.*

A POWERFUL CHALLENGE
TO MY DAILY LIVING

'We will have to repent in this generation not merely for the hateful words and actions of the bad people, but for the appalling silence of the good people.'

Martin Luther King,
in a letter from jail during the early days
of the Civil Rights Movement.

I first read these words many years ago and, every so often, they come back to me as a powerful challenge to my daily living. Am I only making sure that my own life is running on pleasant lines? Do I really care about the violence and poverty that is being inflicted on so many of my sisters and brothers? Have I given up trying to raise my voice because the problems are overwhelming?

I come back not only to Martin Luther King's words, but also to the way in which he lived his short and fruitful life. He refused to be silent in the face of social and moral evil. And he didn't just talk about injustice of course: his words and actions were intermeshed, and profoundly rooted in biblical truth.

As we allow biblical truth to enter our souls, it becomes impossible to sit back and do nothing, however overwhelming the situation and costly our commitment may turn out to be. Our compassion propels us to reach out to human suffering.

Marta Torres, a freedom-fighter and peace activist, wrote, 'Why do we struggle? Two reasons: we struggle because we love and not because we hate, we struggle because our faith in God is alive, not dead.'

'With what shall I come before the Lord, and bow myself before God on high? Shall I come before him with burnt offerings, with calves a year old? Will the Lord be pleased with thousands of rams, with ten thousand rivers of oil? Shall I give my firstborn for my transgression, the fruit of my body for the sin of my soul?' He has told you, O mortal, what is good; and what does the Lord require of you but to do justice, and to love kindness, and to walk humbly with your God?

MICAH 6:6–8

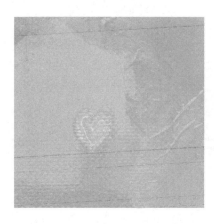

CAN OUR FAITH BE COMFORTABLE?

'Theology for the oppressed women, men and children in India is not an intellectual exploration. It is a daily struggle to understand the meaning of salvation in Christ from a place of alienation, exploitation and shame. It is a theology which aims at liberation through Christ who himself walks with the poor.'

WORDS IN A LETTER FROM A FRIEND IN INDIA

Sometimes in our comfortable, rather bland society, it is easy to forget the massive struggles for justice that go on day by day in our divided world. But the denial of justice to our sisters and brothers is not a reality separate from our own more sheltered lives. We are in this together precisely because Christ's liberation is for all people. And that liberation includes

the right to food, shelter, education, health care and freedom of movement – all the basics we often take for granted. We can be continually
inspired by the number of women and men, who, through their commitment to Jesus, stand for God's righteousness in places of gut-wrenching
oppression and violence.

Can our faith be comfortable if we truly stand in solidarity with those
who fight for justice with their very lives?

Then the King will say to those at his right hand,
'Come, you that are blessed by my Father,
inherit the kingdom prepared for you from the foundation of the world;
for I was hungry and you gave me food,
I was thirsty and you gave me something to drink,
I was a stranger and you welcomed me,
I was naked and you gave me clothing,
I was sick and you took care of me,
I was in prison and you visited me.'

MATTHEW 25:34–36

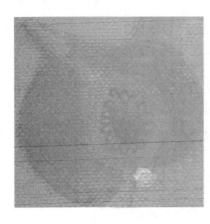

ROOTED IN THE RISEN LORD

A community of pilgrims needs to abandon clutter and to recover fundamentals. It needs to be set free from the obsession with trivia, to discriminate between things that abide, and passing fashions and fads. The sacraments of the pilgrim church deal with basic things – bread, water, oil, the clasp of our sister's and brother's hand. They are the food, provisions and resources for people on the move.

Such a community, rooted and grounded in Christ's resurrection, will be characterised by joy. Not the bogus cheeriness of the hearty, jolly, back-slapping Christians, but the deep joy of those who have attained an inner assurance, a confidence and trust in the power of the risen Christ. A pilgrim church must be a joyful, confident church, which sings the songs of freedom in the midst of bondage. 'Sing Alleluia and keep on walking,' says Augustine in one of his most memorable sermons. As we move into the heart of the storm we will sing but we will keep on walking.

KENNETH LEECH,
writer and community theologian in London

Don't hide,
don't run,
but rather
discover in the midst of fragmentation,
a new way forward,
a different kind of joy,
rooted in the risen Lord.

And walking and singing,
dance at the margins,
and see His face,
where hurt is real
and pain a way of life.

To be alive
in the eye of the storm,
open to Christ's
sometimes uncomfortable peace.

Impossible, you say:
Let me retreat and find my rest.
What rest, my friend,
in these uncertain times?

HAVE WE WALKED
THE WALK?

I am black of skin among whites,
And I am proud,
Proud of race and proud of skin.
I am broken and poor,
Dressed in rags from white man's back,
But I do not think I am ashamed.
Spears could not contend with guns and we were mastered,
But there are things they could not plunder and destroy.
We were conquered but never subservient,
We were compelled but never servile.
Do not think I cringe as white men cringe to whites,
I am proud,
Though humble and poor and without a home ...
So was Christ.

WORDS OF OODGEROO
of the tribe Noonuccal in Australia

Powerful, gut words. Words of strength from a place of oppression. These words define reality in many parts of our divided world. We live in a technological age, but oppressive and dehumanising forces continue to accompany millions of people.

We often speak pious-sounding words about 'being on the side of the poor and standing with the violated'. Yet it is almost impossible for most of us to know what it feels like to be constantly the victim of oppressive structures. We may have talked the talk, but in what sense have we walked the walk?

As we seek God's presence in our daily living, how can we allow truths like those expressed by Oodgeroo actually to change not only our thinking but also the underlying priorities of our lives? It's a huge question – especially as we become more conscious of the economic effects of globalisation on marginalised communities in many countries. It is not a cliché to say 'the poor are getting poorer'. Rather, it is a marker of our times.

Prayer

Companion of the burdened
and liberator of the oppressed,
overturn our easy assumptions
until your wisdom
invades our understanding
each new day.

RETURNING TO GOD

God is here. It is we who have gone out for a walk.

MEISTER ECKHART

Words which are centuries old but as relevant as ever! As my Aboriginal friends in Australia would say: 'We have gone walkabout.' But (unlike my Aboriginal friends) in our journeying we have forgotten that God is with us. We stride out confidently, in our own strength, yet we feel strangely alone at times.

There is a story in Luke's gospel about a young man who had wandered far from his family, and found himself in all kinds of trouble. Then, one day, he decided he would go back to his dad, and on returning home he was welcomed with open arms – loved, embraced, forgiven. Jesus told his followers it was like that with God; that no matter what our failings, there was always a place we could call home. Or to put it another way: in God we become truly ourselves.

Many writers, dramatists and poets lead us on spiritual journeys of huge significance. Through their works they revive the memory of God, often in ways which possess a depth of imagination the churches lack. Writer Nikos Kazantzakis expresses this returning to God powerfully: 'I have one longing only: to grasp what is hidden behind appearance. What is my work? To let the mind fall silent that I may hear the invisible calling.'

The Psalmist put it this way: 'Lord, you are the source of all life, and because of your light, we see the light.' (Psalm 36:9)

Prayer

O Thou who art at home
deep in my heart,
let me loose in Thee
deep in my heart.

FROM A SONG IN THE TALMUD

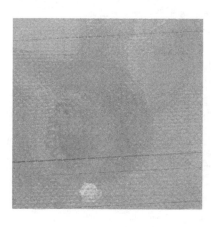

OUR HEARTS STILL SING OF HOPE

Early in the spring of 2003, the war in Iraq began. After watching the first missiles landing on Baghdad, I wrote this poem as I thought about all the suffering that lay ahead for the Iraqi people, and in a sense for us all. And it came powerfully to me that, even in the darkest nights, we cannot live without the possibility of hope – these tiny shoots which unexpectedly spring up through the cracks and truly surprise us.

> *Heard again*
> *in troubled times,*
> *words that speak*
> *of invitation,*
> *of an earthed reawakening,*
> *of surprising resurrection.*
> *Words that, even in these fragile days,*
> *connect us*

with a wider narrative of love,
with a place of transformation,
with a paradigm of grace.

And somewhere
in our souls,
where questions and awareness
meet as friends,
we recognise
that gentle, ancient truth
and,
in this ever-present strength,
discover
that our hearts still sing
of hope.

A king is not saved by his great army;
a warrior is not delivered by his great strength.
The war horse is a vain hope for victory,
by its great might it cannot save …

Our soul waits for the Lord; he is our help and shield.
Our heart is glad in him, because we trust in his holy name.
Let your steadfast love, O Lord, be upon us,
even as we hope in you.

PSALM 33:16–17;20–22

WORDS OF HOPE

Alison is a friend who travels to Palestine to stay with families whose homes are about to be bulldozed by the Israeli army as a security measure. Hundreds of Palestinians have lost their homes, and often their lands, in this massive demolition programme. Yet amidst death, injury, destruction and harassment, Alison also sees another, creative side of human nature.

In one of her letters to friends in Britain she wrote:

> 'It amazes me that so many Palestinians retain a lack of bitterness in view of what they experience. When Abu Mahmoud welcomed us into his home he said, "If the Israeli prime minister were to come here I would offer him tea and cake like any other visitor." That was after the Israeli army had demolished his house and farm in order to extend the security zone or No Man's Land area. Here was a person whose livelihood had been destroyed overnight, along with all he

owned, yet what came over to me was his extraordinary generosity of spirit. I felt so honoured to be with him.'

Abu Mahmoud's incredible lack of bitterness reminded me of a poem by the American peace activist Jojo White. In 1996, twenty-three-year-old Jojo was gunned down as he was walking home from work at Martin Luther King Jr Middle School; his last words to his killer were: 'Peace, brother, One Love.'

Following Jojo's death, his parents helped to fund the 'Break the Silence Mural and Arts Project / Jojo White Solidarity Project'. In 2001, BTS brought Jews and Palestinians together to create a four-story-high mural in Dheisheh Refugee Camp in Bethlehem. On this mural is a poem by Jojo, written when he was just eleven years old. These words (like those of Abu Mahmoud's) are words of hope amidst the barriers and mountain of sorrows which at present cover the land which Jew and Muslim and Christian regard as especially holy. Words of hope for our divided world.

Peace

If I could change the world
I'd dismantle all the bombs
If I could change the world
I would feed all the hungry
If I could change the world
I would shelter all the homeless
If I could change the world
I would make all people free.
I cannot dismantle all the bombs
I cannot feed all the hungry
I cannot shelter all the homeless
I cannot make all people free
I cannot because there is only one of me.
When I have grown and I am strong
I will find many more of me.
We will dismantle all the bombs
We will feed all the hungry
We will shelter all the homeless
We will make all the people free
We will change the world.
Me and my friends
All together, together at last.

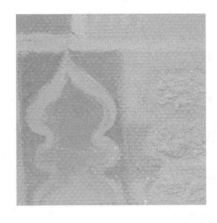

THE CHERISHING OF MEMORIES

I wrote this poem shortly after the very sudden death of my wife, Dorothy, in 2001. Although it reflects my own feelings, I believe the cherishing of memories is universal.

It's the hug,
It's the crazy joke,
It's the warm hand,
It's the fish and chips.

It's the sudden laughter,
It's the silent tears,
It's the high noon,
It's the dark night.

It's the broken bikes,
It's the washing up,
It's the school run,
It's the touch of love.

It's the dog's lick,
It's the loud music,
It's the magic smiles,
It's the stupid dancing.

It's the screaming kids,
It's the loving note,
It's the quick kiss,
It's the great neighbours.

It's the TV switch,
It's the burnt toast,
It's the midnight walk,
It's the lost keys.

It's the local gossip,
It's the easy tenderness,
It's the heart's longing,
It's the morning mist.

It's the hidden pain,
It's the old bracelet,
It's the simple prayer,
It's the long waiting,

It's the truth telling,
It's the searching,
It's the healing,
It's the welcome.

It's the fragility,
It's the strength,
It's the nourishment,
It's the homecoming.

It's the phone,
It's the burst tyre,
It's the washing-up
It's the silly songs.

It's the wisdom.
It's the energy,
It's the hope,
It's the faith.

It's the intimacy,
It's the parting,
It's the tears,
It's the farewell.

It's life,
It's death,
It's the Spirit
Of blessing.

It's the God
Of surprises,
Met again
On the journey.

LIVING WITH QUESTIONS

Be patient toward all that is unsolved in your heart and try to love the *questions themselves* like locked rooms and like books that are written in a very foreign tongue. Do not seek the answers, which cannot be given to you because you would not be able to live them. And the point is, to live everything. *Live* the questions now. Perhaps you will then gradually, without noticing it, live along some distant day into the answer.

RAINER MARIA RILKE

In the months following Dorothy's death, my life was (to say the least) in an unfocused state. In my book *Finding Hope Again*, which I wrote a year after Dorothy's burial, I tried to share some of the various dimensions of grief which I had experienced. After the book's publication, many people wrote to me and shared their own stories of loss and sorrow, and the ways they had journeyed through times of bewilderment and inner dereliction.

A common thread in many of these rich and beautiful stories was the difficulty of living patiently with all the unresolved questions. In this well-known passage from Rilke, the suggestion is made not to seek answers, but rather to live, as calmly as possible, with the questions. Rilke holds to the lived wisdom that, one day, imperceptibly, answers will come.

It is now almost three years since Dorothy's totally unexpected death, and I know something of the truth of that perception.

Lord,
You know the questions in my heart:
the troubling and disturbing ones
that keep me awake at night;
the ones that never seem to go away;
and the ones that reduce me to tears.
Given all this inner turbulence,
I ask you today for a different kind of strength –
a fragment of patience in my soul,
which will enable me to live more calmly
within the confusions of my spirit.

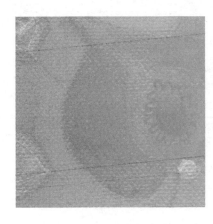

A NEW DEPTH TO
OUR SINGING

I finally understood what Sophie Tucker used to say: 'You have to have your heart broken at least once to sing a love song.'

WORDS OF JAZZ SINGER PEGGY LEE,
who died at 81 in 2002

It may seem like a paradox, but it's true. Authentic joy in life often arises from sorrow. Not always. For suffering can also bring in its wake bitterness and anger and cynicism. Yet when our personal losses enable us to be gentler, more caring human beings, then something very wonderful has happened. And others are also healed by such a transformation in ourselves.

Many of the stories in the New Testament explore this transformational power within suffering. In these stories, Jesus recognises in the many broken-hearted people that he meets, their intimacy with God; that their very tears had carried them into the heart of their Creator's love.

I have learned in my own sorrows not to run from them, but to try to befriend them and to learn from them, even in a small way. That's not always an easy path, but, as strange as it may seem, it can bring a new depth to our singing and to our awareness of God's presence. This simple prayer from Tahiti reminds us of this fact: 'Lord, our palm trees can no longer hide us from the world. Strengthen our hearts that we may look with confidence to the future.'

O Lord …
You have turned my mourning into dancing;
you have taken off my sackcloth
and clothed me with joy,
so that my soul may praise you and
not be silent.
O Lord, my God, I will give thanks
to you for ever.

PSALM 30:10–12

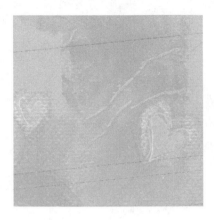

HOW MUCH YOU LOVED

One of the Pharisees asked Jesus to come to his home for lunch and Jesus accepted the invitation. As they sat down to eat, a woman of the streets – a prostitute – heard he was there and brought an exquisite flask filled with expensive perfumes. Going in, she knelt weeping, with her tears falling down upon his feet; and she wiped them with her hair, kissed them and poured the perfume on them.

(LUKE 7:36–38)

In the contradictions of my own life,
where confusion and desire often walk as friends,
I see how much you loved this person,
who in giving her body lived on the margins.

You saw her goodness
when others mocked;
you received her gift
when others sneered;
you touched her body
when others condemned.

And because of that,
I too try to discover
who you are:
the One
who welcomed her,
felt her tears,
disregarded her judges,
and forgave her failures.

Like your friend with the perfume,
I am attracted to you;
drawn by your relaxed acceptance
of difference;
and trusting that you see in me
much more
than a middle-aged bundle of
confused longings,
mixed motives,
half-hearted faith
and pure, downright selfishness.

THE MARKS OF LOVE

There is precious little acceptance in our society
  of the changes in our bodies
  brought about by sacrifice,
  by the giving of life to others.
People want us to look unscathed, unscarred,
  without the sagging in our breasts,
  the stretch marks on our stomach,
  the lines of strain and struggle.
People want us to look ageless, timeless,
  with the model body of a young girl.
  With long, flowing hair,
  fair skin,
  firm upright breasts,
  tight-muscled tummy,
  slim thighs and long legs.
The image of the lithe and slender
  is what men lust for.
The image of what men lust for

is what women strive for.
Where is the place of beauty
    derived from love
    and developed through sacrifice?
Where are the people who will celebrate
    the signs
    of someone
    who has given themself
    to others
    through touch,
    in tears,
    with love,
    unnumbered times?
Who of you will join me
    in forsaking images
    we idolise in society?
Who of you will join me
    in turning away from the mirror
    towards the door
    that leads to the needs of others?
Who of you will join me
    in the risk of being worn out,
    of being wrinkled,
    of being thrown away?
We are not fools,
    who give what we cannot keep
    to gain what we cannot lose.

ANGIE ANDREWS,
Brisbane, Australia

A GLOBAL VISION

Angela died in Madras on Maundy Thursday; she was 39. Although born and brought up in a South Indian home, she had been working as a doctor in London. In October of last year, Angela married John, a Britisher, just a few months after her cancer had been discovered. In February, they both came to Madras to visit Angela's family. It was to be her last journey home, and on Easter Saturday, with a blazing sun high overhead, Angela was buried in the old Christian cemetery, close to the great beach, overlooking the Bay of Bengal. Ten days later, as is the custom here, we had a prayer meeting remembering her life, during which her family played a tape of Angela singing, with great beauty, 'Mary's Boy Child'.

Yet these brief facts convey nothing of the enormous courage with which Angela faced cancer. As she faced this personal battle, she brought strength to all kinds of people – both here in Madras and in London.

When John was with Angela in Madras during the last weeks of her life, he used to worship with us at St Mary's Church. Just after Angela died,

John saw in the church a display of some photographs explaining to visitors how St Mary's Church and a church in Scotland were linked together in the building of a church school in a remote village many miles from Madras city. Before he returned to the UK, we visited this village together and saw the new building, which was to be dedicated a few weeks later. In that desperately poor dalit village – where he was met by many smiling people – John was deeply moved. As he wandered through the narrow, dusty village streets, he thought about his comfortable life in London, and of the contrast between that life and the life he saw here. He was challenged also by the fact that a congregation in far-off Scotland had come forward to share with the local people, and that that sharing and relationship had brought new hope to the whole community.

Two days later, John was back in central London to a new kind of life without Angela. Yet these various experiences in South India – the genuine love of so many strangers which had surrounded him in his sorrow, the atmosphere of serenity and hope that accompanies death in India, the needs of the village people and also their joy – took possession of his heart and mind. He experienced a transformation – that kind of change that comes to many affluent people when they allow their inner life to be touched by the circumstances of the poor, when they are willing to enter into the experience of 'the other'.

Out of that experience, John is now raising money in order that a church school may be built in another village area. In this particular village, the local people had already prepared all the bricks they needed for a new building, but they were never able to afford the other costs involved. Now their hopes are to be fulfilled and the small existing mud church (which every year is damaged by the monsoon) will have beside it a simple, but solid, new building. We can surely say that from sadness has come joy.

The story of Angela and John's involvement in a village here is a sign that human connections in our divided world are still what matter most. What is the ultimate meaning of all our technological and scientific advance if we lose the basic connections among people? We are bundled together on this small planet, not in order to become more isolated and divided – the rich in their corner, the poor in theirs – but so that our understanding of each other may grow and that we may develop a global vision. Again and again, our time in India has taught us that we have so much to learn from each other – rich and poor, Hindu and Christian, villager and city-dweller.

> *Either we walk on the poor and we'll end with Hiroshima,*
> *or we will walk with the poor, which will end in transfiguration.*
> SOURCE UNKNOWN

DOROTHY AND PETER MILLAR
(from *Letters from Madras*, 1988)

OUR WHOLE BEING CRYING OUT FOR THE LIVING GOD

Spirit of
the Living God,
present with us now,
enter you,
body,
mind,
and spirit
and heal you
of all that harms you
in Jesus' name. Amen

FROM THE IONA ABBEY WORSHIP BOOK

This prayer comes from the weekly service of prayer for healing in Iona Abbey. It is spoken during the part of the service when people can receive or share in the ministry of the laying-on of hands.

Each time I read or hear these words, I am reminded of that longing for God which is deep in our hearts. A longing which is itself part of the healing process. Centuries ago, the Psalmist captured this yearning:

> As a deer longs for a stream of cold water, so I long for you, O God.
>
> PSALM 42

And that longing is for God's healing, not just in our bodies, but in our minds and spirits – our whole being crying out for the living God.

Christ's healing touch of divine love and forgiveness reached into the deepest places of people's lives. Even to touch the hem of his garment was a movement towards spiritual and physical integration.

Prayer

Healer of Galilee,
you come again and again
to permeate our human condition;
to take upon yourself our hurts and longings.
Each day you accompany us:
when our bodies are racked with pain,
when our minds are in confusion,
when our failures overwhelm,
when our faith falters,
when our relationships break down,
when loneliness sears our souls.

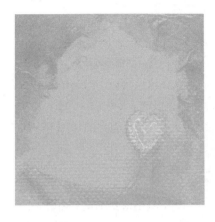

A REVITALISED HUMAN CONSCIOUSNESS ACROSS THE WORLD

Imagine shrinking the earth's population to a village of 100 people
with all the existing human ratios remaining the same.
The village would have 61 Asians, 12 Europeans,
13 North or South Americans, 13 Africans.
One person from Oceania.
There would be 51 females and 49 males.
70 non-whites, 30 whites.
70 non-Christians and 30 Christians.
50% of the village's wealth would be in the hands of 6 people –
all North American citizens.
80 villagers would live in substandard housing;
70 villagers would be unable to read;
while 50 would suffer from malnutrition;
One villager would have a college education.

STATISTICS USED BY MANY INTERNATIONAL AID ORGANISATIONS,
from the 'Global Village e-mail'

We can argue that statistics have a limited value. Yet this particular statistic about our global community underscores both our total interdependence and the tragic divisions within the human family. We may well ask, 'What does God make of it all?' When we consider the world from such a compressed perspective, the need for a creative global vision in each of us becomes glaringly obvious. As one African said, 'While the wealthy nations are heading for outer space, we are still trying to get a decent road to our village.'

Being a member of the Iona Community has taught me to look squarely at these divisions, and to pray and work for a more humane global order. There are millions of us engaged in this task, and that is why 'the people's voice' has become of such significance in international affairs. This voice will not go away in the years ahead, nor will the victims of injustice be silenced. A revitalised human consciousness is developing across the world – a fact which must be pleasing to God, if we take these words from Micah seriously:

> *The Lord has told us what is good.*
> *What he requires of us is this:*
> *To do what is just.*
> *To show constant love.*
> *And to live in humble fellowship with our God.*

> MICAH 6:8

NOT ONLY MYSELF BUT ALSO THIS WORLD

To clasp our hands in prayer is the beginning of an uprising against the world.

THE GREAT TWENTIETH-CENTURY THEOLOGIAN KARL BARTH

Although I have been involved in Christian ministry for more years than I care to remember, I would say that I understand less about prayer and its many dimensions than I did (or thought I did) thirty years ago. That is not to say that I don't believe in prayer, but I certainly couldn't write a manual about it! In my own journey, prayer has so many levels that I find it hard to describe.

Essentially, prayer is about listening to God – that God who inhabits the deepest places of our being. Sheila Cassidy, who helps many people on their spiritual journeys, once wrote:

'When people ask me what I pray for, I say that I don't pray for anything. I pray because God is. I sit before him open like an empty bowl, like a flower, like a wound. I give to God my joy, my confusion, my boredom, my pain – just lay it there on the floor for him to process how he wishes and when he is ready.'

Being open in the way that Sheila Cassidy describes then leads me to name people and situations in my prayers, but the quiet listening comes first. And often I ask myself: Am I, in this place of personal prayer, engaged in a task that can change not only myself but also this world?

Fred Kaan expressed something of Karl Barth's insight in his hymn 'For the healing of the nations':

Lead us forward into freedom;
from despair your world release,
that, redeemed from war and hatred,
all may come and go in peace.
Show us how through care and goodness
fear will die and hope increase.

LEARNING TO LIVE FROM ONE'S DEEP CENTRE

Be still and know that I am God

PSALM 46:10

Many of us around the world are discovering, or re-discovering, the inner strength derived from silent meditation. When our home was in South India, the Benedictine monk Bede Griffiths taught me much about being still and quietly listening to my heart. He believed that Christianity must recover its contemplative traditions, and his life of disciplined prayer touched thousands of people, bringing to their longing for God a greatly enlarged understanding of biblical truth.

Laurence Freeman is another who stands within this tradition of contemplative prayer; he writes about it with poetic grace:

'Meditation is simple and practical. It is about experience rather than theory: a way of being rather than merely a way of thinking. It is a way of living from the deep centre of one's being. Meditation is focused on Christ. This means that it is centred on the prayer of Christ which is continuously poured forth in the Holy Spirit in the depth of each human being. We leave our egotistical self behind to die and rise to our true self in Christ.'

It takes time, practice and determination to live from one's deep centre. Yet according to the Psalmist, it is here that knowledge of God is found. The mysterious, if sometimes restless, currents of our souls carry us into this place of spiritual insight. In the stillness, when our hearts are open, the divine 'can move through', in the words of another guide, Matthew Fox.

I believe that it is in this place that our reverence for scripture, the sacraments and the great Christian traditions of the centuries is deepened.

An exercise

Set down this book, sit comfortably and be still … Allow your thoughts to pass through your mind. Listen in your heart to the words of the psalmist and then enter into a quiet stillness for 10–15 minutes. (At first, this might seem like a long time; after a little practice, though, it will seem too short!)

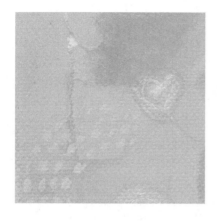

DISCOVERING THE OTHER HALF OF THE SOUL

It was not merely the desire for new ideas which drew me to India, but the desire for a new way of life. I remember writing to a friend at the time: 'I want to discover the other half of my soul.' I had begun to find there was something lacking not only in the Western world but in the Western Church. We were living from one half of our soul, from the conscious, rational level, and we needed to discover the other half, the unconscious, intuitive dimension. I wanted to experience in my life the marriage of these two dimensions of human existence, the rational and intuitive, the conscious and unconscious, the masculine and feminine. I wanted to find the way to the marriage of East and West.

BEDE GRIFFITHS

Velu, who is in his 40s, is badly crippled with leprosy, a disease which is common in the state of Tamil Nadu. Some months ago his wife died.

They had no children. Because of his leprosy, Velu is more or less unemployed, although he does small jobs when he can get them. You might think that, given these outward circumstances, he would be discouraged; but he's far from it. The other day, when I went over to his tiny hut, Velu was busy looking after some neighbours who had come on hard times. His small home was a place of refuge for this family and he had much to give them – not in terms of 'things', for in that sense he has little to share, but in terms of 'being' and 'presence'. In that sense, he has all the riches of the world to offer. And on every street in this overcrowded city there are men and women like Velu. People full of laughter and love, ready, even when they are desperately poor themselves, to go that extra mile for others. People who have much to teach us about 'the other half of the soul'.

India, in all of its contradiction, poverty and complexity, has taught us much about what it means to 'be'. Although it may sound strange to Western ears, in this country 'being' is central to the journey of life. Despite the poverty and oppression, life is still about connections: our connections to each other, our connections to nature and the natural order of things, our connections to the unconscious and the unseen, our connections to the divine. Against this reality, so much of our Western way of life seems rootless, frenetic and empty. Our relationships here in India have not yet become mechanised or clinical. We still seem to know that we are created and not the creators, part and parcel of a great network of being that finds its roots in God's creative power.

To write this about Velu is not for a moment to make light of his crushing poverty. Every day brings him new struggles and frustrations, and on some days it all seems too much to bear. Velu is a victim of injustice and oppression, and his leprosy only makes an already difficult situation more difficult. It is a scandal and an obscenity – in a world which spends so much on 'security'– that the day-to-day trials of Velu only seem to increase. The longer we live here, the more we believe that radical changes must take place within Indian society, and the world, if there is to be any real measure of justice for people like Velu.

In North India, at a community called Anandwan, hundreds of leprosy sufferers are given the possibility of new life. This work of compassion was started by a social worker and visionary, Baba Ampte, whose name is a household word throughout India. Inscribed on a wall at Anandwan are these words:

'I sought for my soul, but my soul failed to see,
I sought my God, but my God eluded me,
I sought my brother, and found all three.'

DOROTHY AND PETER MILLAR
(from *Letters from Madras*, 1988)

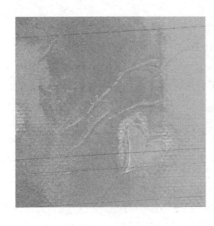

IF WE DO NOT BELIEVE THAT

Let us know,
That highest Lord of Lords,
That highest God of Gods,
The Lord of the world,
The Adorable.

SVETASVATARA UPANISHAD 6:7

It was a great privilege to live for many years in India. As I began to read the Hindu scriptures and to hear them interpreted by wise souls, I found my knowledge of Christ being greatly enlarged. I saw the gospels and their inner truth in a wider frame of meaning. It was an awakening of the spirit which in no way diminished my commitment to the Christian path.

In this verse from the Svetasvatara Upanishad, Hinduism reaches a pure monotheism comparable with that of Isaiah in the Old Testament. The

One who is to be adored is both transcendent and immanent, Creator and Sustainer of the universe, yet dwelling in the heart of every human being – the divine flame within us, sometimes burning brightly, sometimes dimly, but always there. And it is in this place of worship and of adoration that we stand (or sit or kneel) with our sisters and brothers of different faiths. If we do not believe that, our shared human future is bleak.

In these divided times, alive with fear and suspicion of 'the other', God calls us to reach out in love and to take risks; to become more and more conscious that, in seeking to understand other religious traditions, we are, in truth, moving closer to that God whose Light enfolds us all. The Lord of Lords whose image we bear and who, as the old hymn says, 'Holds the whole world in His hands.'

That's the 'whole world' – not just our hemisphere, or our country, or our local parish council. All of us.

O God,
lead us from death to life, from falsehood to truth.
Lead us from despair to hope, from fear to trust.
Lead us from hate to love, from war to peace.
Let peace fill our hearts, our world, our universe.
We ask it for your own name's sake.
Amen

UNIVERSAL PRAYER FOR PEACE
(based on an invocation in Sanskrit)

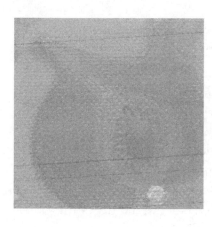

NOT FOR THEM

THE CASSEROLES

If it had been Three Wise Women instead of Three Wise Men, they would have:

1. Asked directions
2. Arrived on time
3. Helped deliver the baby
4. Cleaned the stable
5. Brought practical gifts
6. Made a casserole

WORDS IN A LETTER FROM FRIENDS,
from a joke circulating on the Internet

We may not agree entirely with these humorous words, but I think they hold a few truths! When we lived in India, many overseas visitors stayed in our home. They came from a wide variety of traditions, faiths and cultures. Among these many pilgrims were some who were totally in love with a romantic notion of the great sub-continent. Its legends, its spirituality, its multiple passions enthralled them. But when we came to discuss practical things like poverty and injustice, they floated off. Not for them the casseroles, or rather the lack of them.

At the heart of life there will always be a place for the romantic spirit, and I like to think I possess something of that ingredient in my own life. Yet in every situation, someone has to cook the food and wash the dishes. These words about the Wise Women underline the practical nature of the Christian faith. Or to put it differently – it's often in the cooking and dish washing that we discover the blessing of Christ's presence. My Celtic forebears understood this well, as is obvious from their prayers and blessings which are grounded in the ordinary events of each day (milking the cow, lighting the fire). In the words of an old prayer:

> *Christ the carpenter,*
> *help us to get our hands dirty as we work for you.*

IN REALITY, ALL THAT WE HAVE

Monks, what is the noble truth
about the way that leads to the cessation of suffering?
Just this noble eightfold way:
namely, right view, right purpose,
right speech, right action,
right livelihood, right effort,
right mindfulness and right concentration.

THE BUDDHA

In Australia, where I have recently been living, Buddhism is the fastest growing religion. On several occasions, I have had the privilege of discussing our journeys in the Spirit with the monks at the great Buddhist temple some miles south of Sydney. I am particularly attracted by the importance of 'right mindfulness' within the eightfold path – its counsel of attending to all that is present in the moment; in the here and now.

Often our scattered minds throw us back into the past, or propel us into the unknowable future; yet how important it is in our spiritual quest to cherish and celebrate the present, which is, in reality, all that we have. Jesus reminds us again and again in his teaching of the preciousness of the moment, of the divine revelation in the midst of daily living. There is a Jewish saying that I love: 'Every moment is a door through which the Messiah may enter.'

Buddhist meditation is helping many people to centre their minds on the present, and the growing worldwide interest in Christian meditation is illumining a similar path. Genuine mindfulness is not something that can be achieved in a few days or a few weeks. Rather, it is a life-long pilgrimage into awareness. And in our interconnected world, there are many authentic guides who can walk alongside us as we seek to centre our lives upon the things that ultimately matter.

Once Jesus was asked by the Pharisees when the kingdom of God was coming, and he answered, 'The kingdom of God is not coming with things that can be observed; nor will they say, 'Look, here it is!' or 'There it is!' For, in fact, the kingdom of God is among you.'

LUKE 17:20–21

Prayer

Neither eight hundred years ago, nor yesterday
are these our flesh and bones redeemed;
but now in this moment
as we put our trust in Thee
we are made new,
new creatures we become.
The inner flesh of our immortal bodies – vibrant to eternity.

GEORGE MACLEOD

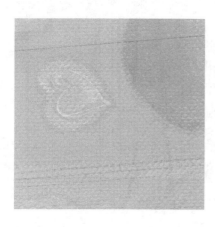

WILL WE EVER LEARN?

You're not even a number any more, you're a bar code.

DAVIE McCUISH,
quoted in Fergal Keane's *Forgotten Britain*

Is Davie's observation correct? In the midst of our affluence are we all merely bar codes? Numbers on a giant computer. Statistics for some government department.

I think that many people feel this to be true, for society as a whole seems concerned only with money, status and power. If you don't possess any of these, it's easy to feel totally marginalised; and many people are in that place.

The Iona Community, since its early days in the 1930s, has tried, often falteringly, to walk alongside those who feel worthless and abandoned in society. That accompaniment is just as important today as it was seventy years ago. Within post-modern societies there are new forms of abandonment and many of these have exceptionally cruel faces. People don't just feel like bar codes, they are treated as such.

And it is exactly here that any proclamation of the Christian position must emphasise its counter-cultural truth: that the marginalised matter to God; that those who feel excluded and vulnerable and worthless are close friends of Jesus; that there is an upside down Kingdom full of surprises, including the fact that the very least will be at the top table.

People valued for who they are and not for what they possess. Will we ever learn?

Do not fear, for I have redeemed you;
I have called you by name, you are mine.
When you pass through the waters, I will be with you;
and through the rivers, they shall not overwhelm you;
when you walk through fire you shall not be burned,
and the flame shall not consume you …
Because you are precious in my sight,
and honoured, and I love you.

ISAIAH 43:1–4

LISTENING TO THE POOR

Lord, you are the God of all Europeans, all Americans, all Asians …
you are also my God – me, an African – me, a Beninois.

Lord,
I want to sing, dance and look radiant with happiness.
But alas the wars on my continent,
AIDS, poverty and malaria
are destroying my brothers and my sisters.
Instead of joy, there is sadness, fear, sorrow and anxiety.

Lord,
I am confused but not downtrodden
because for me, an African, a Beninois,
you are my God and Jesus your Son,
who died and rose for me, is my Saviour.
He is my eternal hope.

Pastor Raphael Houessou

For me this is both the miracle and mystery of the Christian faith: Raphael comes from Benin, one of the poorest countries within a desperately poor continent; daily, in his pastoral work, he witnesses the ravages of disease and mind-blowing poverty. Would not such a situation destroy a person's faith in God?

Cynics might say that Raphael was a 'simple man with a simple faith'. I don't believe that for a moment, and believe it even less having myself lived alongside communities burdened with poverty. In Raphael, and many others around the world, we see clear evidence of a confidence in God which has largely been lost within the bland dimensions of Christianity in affluent societies. For Raphael, faith in Christ is not an additional extra within the pluralities of life. It is life. Or perhaps more accurately, it is both life and death.

Raphael has much to teach us about what it means to be a follower of Jesus. Yet we are reluctant students! We, who belong to the rich and powerful global club, have little time, even in our churches, to listen to the oppressed of the earth. We forget that, in terms of understanding the miracle and mystery of Christianity, they may be much more knowledgeable. A truth expressed beautifully in this letter from a Canadian friend in Cotonou, Benin:

> ... *It's amazing the way people here dress in such beautiful, bright colours! Market women in kerchiefs and colourful pagnés (long wrap-around skirts) selling piles of ripe mangos, oranges, bananas, red onions, tomatoes ... Beautiful, ebony women swathed in such deep, rich, infinite colour – indigo, turquoise,*

ultramarine, French blue, ruby, wine, crimson, copper, coral, terra cotta, rust, lemon, canary, amber, ochre, saffron …

A woman in a vibrant green pagné: Green as the pyramid of unripe oranges she balances on a tray on her head; green as the sound of a family of parrots sharing a rattan-wicker cage; green as piles of corn husks on the red-brown earth; green as the puddles of truck effluent the woman steps around, head held high.

Men sometimes wear a 'costume' called a 'grand boubou', which is a robe-like garment with pants and a shirt underneath – some patterns geometric; others kaleidoscopic; some all flowery or leafy; others covered in whorls and spirals; others swimming all over with stylised fish, coral, wavy sea plants …

Some grand boubous intricately and richly embroidered with gold thread around the neck and big sleeves.

Some simply one, solid colour – it depends on the occasion. A man in a solid-blue grand boubou. Like the ocean on a motorbike.

Amazing! All of this colour and design against the background of a grim, ugly city – rotting piles of garbage, malarial mud, rusty tin shacks, hoardings for undertakers, thick black clouds of carbon monoxide choking everyone, dulling everything.

The infinite colours and patterns: the reflection of a rich culture, a fertile imagination, a deeply rooted connection to the land and *sea; a land that, by the minute, is being cleared of trees (palms, acacias, baobabs) to supply people with some charcoal to cook over; a spot of warmth against the (surprisingly) cold night. You can smell the bush fires when the wind is blowing a certain way – like the acrid, smoky breath of an apocalyptic beast who brings desert, lumbering closer and closer.*

The infinite colours and design: the reflection of the Spirit of a people who cannot be crushed – not by slavery, not by the colonialism, not by the brutal structural 'adjustment' programmes of the World Bank and IMF ... There is an incredible resilience to people here. An irrepressible sense of fun and humour in the ways the children and gossiping market women tease me. An aristocratic dignity, and fierce proudness, in the high-boned faces of burdened women stepping elegantly around raw sewage and truck effluent.

I am a white man – white as enriched, imported French flour; I am respected for my money, knowledge, experience ... I am not rich. I am not wise. I am not developed: secure in my first-world privilege, locked in my Landrover, protected by my mefloquine, bottled water, credit card, open ticket ... What experience do I possess of living with death every day, of creative survival, of incredible good-humoured patience, of real hope, of dazzling resurrection? I feel like a child here. What do I have to teach these people? I have the world to learn from them! ...

THE RAINBOWS IN OUR MIDST

Forgive us that narrowness of vision
which sees only the clouds
and misses the rainbows

WORDS FROM A GROUP OF WOMEN IN GUATEMALA

When I was working in the Diocese of Madras (now Chennai) in South India, I remember one humid afternoon in rural Tamil Nadu. With the local pastor, I was crossing in a small, frail boat to a village where most of the thatched homes had been washed away in the monsoon rains a couple of days earlier. As I crossed the water, I was wondering what on earth I was going to say to the villagers who had suffered greatly. I need not have worried. After the initial greetings, the villagers smilingly told us that God had been so good to them! They then went on to say that no one had died in the floods, and that they still had a chicken and some rice for our supper. And then, in the wonderful tradition of Indian Christianity, the villagers immediately, in prayer, thanked God for our safe arrival in their midst.

It was in these South Indian villages, which to the outside observer may appear primarily as places of gut-wrenching poverty, that I began to learn a little about seeing the rainbows, rather than the clouds. The villagers' optimism was never superficial nor grounded in fatalism. Rather, it was the product of a deep spirituality which intuitively recognised that God's presence permeated every aspect of life.

It is often from places of suffering, uncertainty and apparent hopelessness that Christ's hope announces itself. That may be a paradox, but from my own experience of living in situations of material poverty, I believe it is true. And sometimes, in our affluence, we need to be forgiven for missing the rainbows in our midst. They are there! Look around.

THE 'DEVELOPED' WORLD – 'NEITHER COLD NOR HOT'

Many young people from the Western world pass through our home in Madras. They usually come from what many in India think of as the 'developed world'. As we share with them, we discover time and again that they long to do something really meaningful with their lives. They want to 'reach out'. And very often they want to do this reaching out with a great deal of love and compassion. They want to be affected by the cries of the poor, not just to pass by on the other side of the street. They want to sit where the poor sit and share their journey. They do not want merely a 'comfortable life' – the kind described in the Book of Revelation as 'neither cold nor hot'. They want to be challenged and they want their life to have depth.

But as we discuss more, their pain is also revealed. And it *is* pain. For many of these affluent people from the West feel that it is impossible to touch such depths of life in their own harshly materialistic society. There, in a world dominated by tacky, tawdry consumerism, everything seems so clinical; they cannot find humanity. That heartbeat, which seems to be everywhere in a country like India, is absent. Death, sorrow, joy and disappointment are all shoved in a corner so that the 'good life' may reign. All that matters is the outward show – what we have and not who we are. In the West, we have become obsessed with protecting our possessions; if only we can keep our things secure life will be fine. The ultimate protection of our things is spelt out clearly in our defence budgets.

DOROTHY AND PETER MILLAR
from *Letters from Madras*, 1988

Prayer

O God, strengthen us in our desire,
and breathe into our bodies the passion of your love.

THE IONA ABBEY WORSHIP BOOK

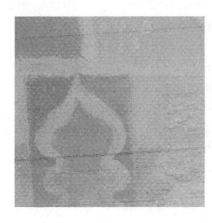

UNLESS WE CAN LISTEN
TO OTHER CULTURES

May the rains fall on our land
And the cows grow fat.
May the children take the wisdom of the ancestors
And build on all that is good.
May time stand still
As we gaze upon the beauty that is around us.
And may the love in our hearts,
Envelop all those whom we touch.

A ZULU PRAYER

I read this prayer through a couple of times and then sit in silence – my heart alive both to its healing possibilities and to its challenge. It is a prayer which many would think of as coming from 'a poor part' of the world, and certainly that is true in purely material terms. But think of the vast spiritual riches in which a prayer like this is earthed.

It reminds us of a wholeness – an integrated way of seeing life – and in that sense it is closer to biblical wisdom than many of our own rather domesticated prayers which often limit God. These beautiful Zulu words illumine a wider canvas. Linked to the good earth, which we are rapidly polluting, they then take us back into our heritage and its accrued truths. Yet they don't leave us there, but carry us into a place of gentle silence before encouraging us to be a people of love in our own time and place.

For me this prayer is an amazing combination of profound theology and practical Christianity, and it confirms my belief that unless we can listen to other cultures and to their knowledge of Christ, we are truly impoverished. Mother Teresa of Calcutta expressed that truth in simple words:

> *Grant that with your love,*
> *I may be big enough to reach the world,*
> *and small enough to be one with you.*

RELIGIOUS LANGUAGE

May the raindrops fall lightly upon your brow,
May the soft winds freshen your spirit,
May the sunshine brighten your heart,
May the burdens of the day rest lightly upon you,
And may God enfold you in the mantle of his love.

A Gaelic blessing

For as long as I can remember I have loved this prayer. In dark days it has given me courage to go on, and in less dark ones it has enabled my spirit to touch into the greatness and goodness of God. I have also noticed over several years that when I use this prayer, in a church service or at a meeting, people often ask for a copy of the words, which they then pass on to friends.

Yet there is another reason why this prayer means a lot to me. Some of my time is spent with folk for whom institutional religion has little, if any, meaning. Of course this does not mean that they are not seeking God. Many who find themselves far outside the churches are on profound spiritual journeys, and a blessing such as this is an authentic connecting point with the creator and sustainer of all life. An entry point to faith.

That is special. And the churches must continue to reflect on why such prayers as this can touch right into the centre of people's lives; people who perhaps carry no 'religious language', but who immediately feel connected to God and to the world through such words. Is it because a blessing like this carries the sense that life and nature and God and people – in all of their incredible beauty and pain and variety – are to be celebrated? That God's love surrounds us, and that everything is threaded through with love?

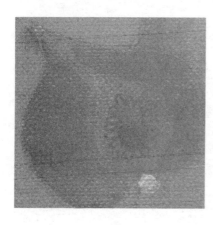

REAL SANCTITY

The real sanctity of a church is that it is a place where we can
go to weep and laugh in common.

MIGUEL DE UNAMUNO

The great Indian poet Rabindranath Tagore wrote: 'While God waits for
his temple to be built of love, people bring stones.'

It is easy for our churches to become formalised, rigidly structured places
where we can never reveal our real pain and the desires of our hearts.
Often we are more human outside churches than inside!

Yet in many poor congregations around the world, often in places of
desperate hardship, I have discovered the real sanctity that Miguel de

Unamuno writes about – sacred places where authentic openness to God occurs as congregations weep and laugh and argue and sing together, where people share their humanity in all of its amazing plurality, messiness and beauty.

> *Lord, bring to our house your pain,*
> *that sharing it we may also share your joy;*
> *bring to our house all those*
> *who hurry or hobble behind you,*
> *that we may meet you as the saviour of all.*

ADAPTED FROM THE IONA ABBEY WORSHIP BOOK

To recognise Christ in our brothers and sisters, to be human and 'real' together, to share our tears and joys, is not this the meaning of church?

'God is our shelter and strength,' wrote the psalmist.

Prayer

Jesus, teach us to accept each other as you accept us –
in our differences, in our awkwardnesses, in our peculiarities –
that a building of God may be firmly made
out of different-shaped stones.
Enable us to accept one another just as we are,
not trimmed into smooth conformities.

ADAPTED FROM A PRAYER BY IAN FRASER

SHANTI'S JOURNEY

Just beyond our front gate, many of the main roads in Madras meet together. The place is called 'Gemini flyover' and there is hardly a moment in the day when it is not crowded with lorries, buses, cars, bullock-carts, motorbikes, autoricks, cycles, handcarts and hundreds of people. In other words, it is a busy place! To stand at Gemini for even a couple of minutes is to experience Indian life in all of its myriad contradiction and infinite variety. To a stranger it may be overwhelming – a sea of humanity moving in a thousand different directions all at once.

The other morning as I came round the flyover on my bike, I saw two small figures right at the heart of all the confusion – Shanti and her son, Arun, on their way to the local bazaar. Within a few seconds I lost sight of them, but in that fleeting moment on the roundabout so many parts of Shanti's journey during these past few years came to my mind. Negotiating the Gemini flyover was for Shanti and Arun as nothing compared to their daily struggle for food and shelter.

I first met Shanti in church, early on a weekday morning. She was sitting quietly meditating and she told me that she always found a great sense of peace within the old and familiar church. Yet after she had told me her story, I could not help thinking that Shanti (whose name means 'peace') needed many more things in addition to peace of mind. Shortly after Arun's birth, Shanti's husband left her for another woman and never returned. She found a tiny room to rent and worked for the next few years in a factory. Her wage was small, but neighbours offered to look after Arun. Despite this support, it was a terrible struggle and often Shanti went without food, especially if it was towards the end of the month when her wages had run out. Then suddenly the factory closed and Shanti was unemployed.

She was able to get small jobs from time to time, but as Arun grew older the struggle to make ends meet increased. Then her health broke down and there was no income. They moved out onto the pavement where there was no rent to pay, but also no roof over their heads. Shanti's family, poor themselves, could give little help. So the long journey through the Madras streets began – the search for a job, any job, and for daily food. Amazingly, through it all, Arun kept going to school and did well in his studies. Shanti, even in the face of so much discouragement, seemed to find fresh strength – and another job.

It would be so good to say that Shanti's struggles are over, but that is far from the case. Certainly she has a job (it brings in about 13 pounds sterling a month) and a small room in a crowded slum area. Yet to survive on such a small income in a city like Madras, where prices have risen enormously in recent years, is almost impossible, and the years ahead will bring more uncertainty for them both.

That is one side of the picture. The other side is the way in which they have faced up to these daily battles for survival. To meet with Shanti and Arun is not to meet with bitter or cynical people. Despite their toil and anxiety, they carry within themselves that quiet dignity and inner peace which is characteristic of so many desperately poor people. They can still laugh; they can still share what little they have with others. They have so much to teach us and we count it a privilege to be their friends. From Shanti and Arun we have learned many lessons about ourselves – not least of which is that our own comfortable life is very often rooted in a real lack of compassion for others.

The story of Shanti and Arun is the story of millions of our brothers and sisters around the world; and there are far more Shantis and Aruns in the world than at any time before. Yet, in our folly, we continue to spend billions of dollars every year on weapons of war to protect our affluence. How much more sane it would be if we could listen to the poor and stand beside them. Our understanding of security would be transformed. We could begin to move together – rich and poor – on a journey of compassion.

Many generations ago, St Francis of Assisi, whose heart and mind had been transformed because of his sharing with the poor of his time, expressed all of this with immense clarity in these amazing words:

> O Divine Master,
> grant that I may not so much seek
> to be consoled as to console,
> to be understood as to understand,
> to be loved as to love.

For it is in giving that we receive,
it is in pardoning that we are pardoned,
and it is in dying that we are born again
to eternal life.

Such words have a new force and depth amidst the injustices of our own time. We cannot be comfortable when there are so many Shantis and Aruns around us, but we can be something more significant: sharers in their journey, and learners from their lives.

DOROTHY AND PETER MILLAR
(from *Letters from Madras*, 1988)

EARTH'S MUSIC

Great Spirit,
Give us hearts to understand,
Never to take
From creation's beauty
More than we can give.

Never to destroy wantonly
For the furtherance of greed.

Never to deny to give our hands
For the building of earth's beauty.
Nor to take from her
What we cannot use.

Give us hearts to understand,
That to destroy

Earth's music
Is to create confusion.

That to wreck
Her appearance
Is to blind us to beauty.

That to callously
Pollute her fragrance
Is to make
A house of stench.

That as we care for her
She will
Care for us.

United Nations Environmental Sabbath Programme

We cannot be 'a friend of the earth' on our own. We need each other as we seek to listen attentively to the increasingly distraught cries of our wounded planet. And we need also the wisdom of those who have walked, through the centuries, in harmonious companionship with the earth, like the Yoruba people in West Africa. Here is their voice:

Enjoy the earth gently,
enjoy the earth gently;
for if the earth is spoiled
it cannot be repaired.
Enjoy the earth gently.

Against Our Mesmerising Scientific Achievements

Born in poverty
Died in custody
In an age of technology

Aboriginal poster in Brisbane, Australia

In the past few years I have had the privilege of working alongside the Wellspring Community, an ecumenical Christian community in Australia involved in, among many other issues, reconciliation with indigenous communities. I have found this part of Wellspring's work truly inspiring, for it is a complex task. As one Aboriginal elder said to me, 'As a white person your job is to listen and learn, and then listen to us more.'

It was on the wall of a glittering office block in downtown Brisbane that I first saw this poster. Since that spring morning in that beautiful city, I have read it countless times, and each time it strikes me with new force. It is a message, not only from the Aboriginal people of Australia, but from the many parts of our wounded world. It is a cry from the very heart of our shared humanity. Against the edifice of our mesmerising scientific achievements and vast global wealth, a message like this stops us short in our tracks. It reaches our souls – and that's exactly its purpose.

Across the barriers that divide race from race,
Across the barriers that divide rich from poor,
Across the barriers that divide people of different cultures and faiths,
Reconcile us, O Christ, by your cross.

A PRAYER FROM THE WORLD COUNCIL OF CHURCHES

A VAST CANVAS
OF MEANING

We look up and see the stars shining above.
And we say, 'They are the bright suns
and around them are the planets,
possibly with people we will never see.'
However, when my
Aboriginal people looked up
at the night sky they didn't
see the stars – they never saw stars.
They only saw
the campfires of their ancestors
on their journey.
The bright stars were the ancestors
who were not long gone;
the dimmer stars were the ancestors
further on the journey.

WORDS OF EDDIE KNEEBONE, AN ABORIGINAL ELDER

It has been a huge privilege to have had the opportunity to live alongside Aboriginal communities in various parts of Australia. To say that it has been an enriching experience would be to completely understate something very special.

When I am with Aboriginal friends, I am always conscious of that vast canvas of meaning, narrative, sacredness and tradition which is their inheritance.

Within Aboriginal understanding, spirituality and the natural world are inseparable, and the past makes sense of the present. Our often rather fragile immediacies (what we see now is all there is) are incomprehensible to an Aboriginal mind – which is one reason why there is such a wounding clash of cultures in Australia.

The wisdom of indigenous understanding and its wider canvas of meaning has much to teach us about the search for an authentic spirituality. But it is my conviction that we need to engage on our search not outside but within the often confusing pluralities of our modern culture. It is tempting to try to escape into some form of romantic idealism. Our re-informed capacity for wonder, mystery and the sacred must find its roots in the ordinary, and sometimes difficult, events of each new day.

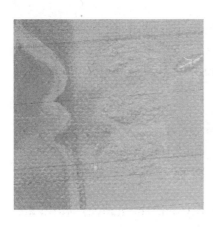

THE BIG PICTURE

The only way to eat an elephant is in small pieces.

WORDS USED BY ARCHBISHOP DESMOND TUTU OF SOUTH AFRICA

I think these words originally come from an old African proverb, but whatever their source they speak to us all. Laughter-making and thought-provoking at the same time, simple and profound, these words cut through all of our obsessive planning for the unknowable future and remind us that whatever lies at hand or ahead, we can, in actual fact, only take one step at a time.

In some ways, these words are quite like some of the sayings of Jesus. They bring me back to Christ's teaching in the Sermon on the Mount (words much loved by many Hindus, I discovered when I was living in South India).

In the Sermon on the Mount, Jesus outlines a multi-levelled pathway for living in a gentle and authentic companionship with God, with the natural world, and with one another.

One of the reasons why many of us are stressed out is because we are not content unless we see the whole picture. Yet throughout the Bible we are constantly reminded of the preciousness of the moment – of each new day. We will never see the big picture or discern the great purposes of God through time and eternity, but we can be present to each new day, each new situation, each person that we met. This moment, with all of its possibilities, is a rich and wonderful small piece.

Therefore I tell you, do not worry about your life, what you will eat or what you will drink, or about your body, what you will wear. Is not life more than food, and the body more than clothing? Look at the birds of the air; they neither sow nor reap nor gather into barns, and yet your heavenly Father feeds them. Are you not of more value than they? And can any of you by worrying add a single hour to your span of life? And why do you worry about clothing? Consider the lilies of the field, how they grow; they neither toil nor spin, yet I tell you, even Solomon in all his glory was not clothed like one of these. But if God so clothes the grass of the field, which is alive today and tomorrow is thrown into the oven, will he not much more clothe you – you of little faith? Therefore, do not worry saying, 'What will we eat?' or 'What will we drink?' or 'What will we wear?' For it is the Gentiles who strive for all these things; and indeed your heavenly Father knows that you need all these things. But strive first for the kingdom of God and his righteousness, and all these things will be given to you as well.

So do not worry about tomorrow, for tomorrow will bring worries of it own. Today's trouble is enough for today.

MATTHEW 6:25–34

TO SEE YOUR WORLD WITH INFORMED AWARENESS

Worldwide 800 million people are living in chronic hunger.
(WORLD WATCH INSTITUTE)

2 billion people are undernourished.
(ECOGROWTH + INEQUITY)

One fifth of the world's population receives 83% of the world's income. The poorest fifth receives 1.5%.
(BREAD FOR THE WORLD INSTITUTE)

3 billion people in the world live on less than $2 a day. 20% of the world live on less $1 a day.
(WORLD BANK)

130 million children have no access to basic primary education.
(UNICEF)

Every year millions of people are reduced to grinding poverty because up to 40% of their country's income is spent on servicing foreign debt.
(JUBILEE DEBT CAMPAIGN)

God of everyone on earth,
how do I respond
to these
grim statistics?

Do I beg for mercy,
or send money to Oxfam,
or change my lifestyle,
or work in Africa,
or say more prayers,
or campaign,
or write letters,
or become cynical,
or drug myself stupid,
or … or … or …?

I am confused, uncertain,
inwardly restless.

Yet in my calmer moods,
I sense this discomfort
is one of your
surprising gifts in my life –
opening my eyes
to see your world
with informed awareness:
to walk with greater tenderness upon your earth.

BONE OF OUR BONE...

More than 11 million children in sub-Saharan Africa have now lost one or both parents to Aids, and the fast-rising death toll suggests that within seven years the number will have climbed to 20 million, says UNICEF, the UN children's organisation ...

Without parental protection and support, orphans are at risk of malnutrition and exploitation, as well as losing out on education. Many face discrimination from those who think that orphans may have been infected with HIV.

About 90% of orphans are cared for – often with great difficulty – by their extended families. The number of children living on the streets with no adult to protect them is rising in many sub-Saharan cities.

If one parent dies, a child's suffering is often worsened because the household income drops and the child may be taken out of school to look after the surviving parent, or to try to earn money ...

Many of the severely affected countries have no policies and little money to help the orphans. 'Their reluctance also reflects a lingering unease about HIV/Aids itself,' it [the UNICEF report] adds.

FROM A REPORT IN THE GUARDIAN
about a 2003 UNICEF report on HIV/Aids in Africa

And they were bringing children to him, that he might touch them; and the disciples rebuked them. But when Jesus saw it he was indignant, and said to them, 'Let the children come to me, do not hinder them; for to such belongs the kingdom of God. Truly, I say to you, whoever does not receive the kingdom of God like a child shall not enter it.' And he took them in his arms and blessed them, laying his hands upon them.

MARK 10:13–16

In the light of Christ's words, the almost unbelievable suffering of millions of young children is hard to comprehend. In fact, we cannot comprehend it.

Faced with such a reality can we touch more deeply into this state of incomprehension in ourselves? Dom Helder Camara, who was for years a saint of the marginalised in his native Brazil, used the phrase 'the uncomfortable peace of Christ'. In relation to the children in Africa something of this discomfort must become part of our spirituality. In a real sense, these kids who are suffering are our own kids. In the mystery of creation, they are bone of our bone and flesh of our flesh, and their cries resound in our souls. Our destiny in God is inseparable from theirs – a fact which should make a real difference to our daily living, and to theirs!

CHRIST OF GETHSEMANE

During the recent civil war in his country, a young person in a village in the poverty-stricken eastern part of Sierra Leone was chatting to a visiting white priest. Many of his family and friends had been killed or tortured. The diamond mines had become a central focus of the war.

'What do you white people do with diamonds?' asked the young man.

'Well,' said the priest, 'women like to wear them.'

There was a pause, then: 'And just for that we are killing each other?'

Christ of Gethsemane,
I can easily be overwhelmed
by all the violence and greed in your world,
but even in my powerlessness
I know
that today
you are especially close to
all who are

    cheated
    betrayed
    exploited
    bullied
    enslaved
    tyrannised
    abused
    persecuted
    silenced
    driven from home
    robbed
    violated
    detained without trial
    imprisoned
    held hostage
    tortured.

IN THESE FRAGILE TIMES

Pentecost did not happen the day after Easter. Perhaps resurrection takes a bit of getting used to. Instead, the disciples waited and prayed. And suddenly, without warning, they were filled with power. At a time like this, filled with huge preventable suffering, we look for the freeing of the Spirit. We pray for the peace of the world. We ask, give us Pentecost again. And, like the disciples, we cannot predict where or when or how the Spirit will move among us. But we can wait in hope and readiness, open to its coming.

KATHY GALLOWAY,
Leader of the Iona Community

How do we wait
in these fragile times?

How do we understand
resurrection
in the face of so much death?

How can we be still
when so many around
are violated?

Questions
that we cannot answer –
just like the disciples of old.

They were baffled too,
and lost,
weary with grief.

Yet with them
we can pray:

God, in these fragile times,
help us to remain open to your Spirit,

to work
for the coming of peace and understanding
in our violent and divided world.

AT THE HEART OF HUMAN EXPERIENCE

As we look round at our world, so many things could cause us to despair and feel helpless. The arms trade increases every day; millions upon millions are starving in many countries. Across the world, poor people are denied even the basic rights of life. All of this is a fact, and to close our eyes to it is to cease to be a human being.

One night, when I was feeling very burdened about all this sad news, I opened the Bible and read these words:

> *He unrolled the scroll and found the place where it is written:*
> *'The Spirit of the Lord is upon me, because he has chosen me to*
> *bring good news to the poor. He has sent me to proclaim liberty*
> *to the captives and recovery of sight to the blind; to set free the*
> *oppressed and announce that the time has come when the Lord*
> *will save his people.'*

Jesus rolled up the scroll, gave it back to the attendant and sat down. All the people in the synagogue had their eyes fixed on him, as he said to them, 'This passage of scripture has come true today, as you heard it being read.'

And with millions of others in the world today, I believe that these words of Jesus are true; that Jesus Christ did come into the world in order that men and women in every generation should find hope and light; that he did bring good news. As he spoke these words from Isaiah 61, Jesus was not speaking of some wonderful, remote world someplace else. He was speaking about our world – full of human problems and sadness, tragedy and brokenness. He was not speaking about some comfortable, easy life, but about poverty, oppression and struggle of many kinds. It was within this world of human suffering that Jesus announced a new kingdom. Is that not surprising? Is it not amazing? Is it not absolute foolishness?

From now on, God was to work right at the heart of human experience, and to work in such a way that the pain of our world became his own pain. God in a wonderful way had entered human history and come to share human experience.

The theologian Leonardo Boff wrote: 'God does not give an answer to all our questions, but enters into the heart of them all.'

Many years ago in Lima, Peru a small group who were working with prisoners brought together a collection of contemporary psalms called 'Psalms for Life and Peace'. This psalm, based on psalm 88, powerfully mirrors the wisdom of Isaiah 61:

God, freedom for the oppressed,
Christ, our liberator,
from deep within our prisons
we cry to you; hear our lament.
Take note of our protest
for we are held captive.
Break the circle of death
that keeps us wounded.
Come down to the darkness
of this hell.
We are alone, gagged, hungry.
But despite the chains
of this captivity,
life still throbs
and we keep on living.

RECONNECTED WITH THE ENERGIES OF GOD

Lord, in these times,
when we feel that we are losing hope
or feel that our efforts are futile,
let us see in our hearts and minds
the image of your resurrection,
and let that be our source of courage and of strength.
With that, and in your company,
help us to face our challenges and struggles
against all that is born of injustice.

This simple prayer comes from the Philippines. Its power lies in its universal significance. We ourselves may not be up against the massive injustices which mark the lives of our sisters and brothers in many parts of the world, but we can all identify with the loss of hope and the feeling that our efforts are futile.

Yet this particular prayer has always had great meaning for me because it intimately relates these all too common feelings of hopelessness with the image of Christ held in our being. Yes, we experience situations where all seems lost, but at that very place of abandonment, we can be reconnected with the energies of God.

Centuries ago, the prophet Isaiah expressed this truth in some amazing words:

> *Those who trust in the Lord for help*
> *will find their strength renewed.*
> *They will rise up on wings like eagles;*
> *they will run and not get weary;*
> *they will walk and not grow weak.*
>
> ISAIAH 40:31

BEING OBEDIENT TO GOD'S LAW

Lord,
Give me the desire
to obey your laws
rather than to get rich.
Keep me from
paying attention
to what
is worthless.

PSALM 119:36–37

A strong plea indeed. No fooling around here. These words come from the longest psalm, and in one translation come under the heading 'A prayer for understanding'. The psalmist is engaged in an intense spiritual quest, seeking to move closer to his Creator's design for humanity. Central to his search is the longing to be obedient to the divine law. (Psalm 119:23–40)

But what an extraordinary, if barely attainable, possibility for people within affluent communities! To follow the ways of God instead of chasing after money and its many manifestations? 'Help me steer clear of worthless things,' the psalmist sings. A tall order in our tinsel-decked society where celebrity and appearance constantly count for so much more than substance.

A biblical text such as this raises for me the question: How do we actually implement such teachings in our daily lives? When every social marker around us points us in another direction, can we live in a counter-cultural space and still be connected to modern realities? Two of the Rules of the Iona Community provide me with something of a touching place in relation to the Psalmist's cry: these are 'accounting for the use of our time' and 'accounting for the use of our money'. Like most of us, though, I still have a long way to go in being even momentarily obedient to God's law. How about you?

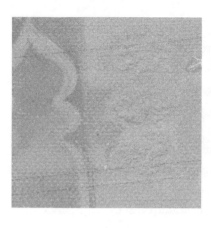

POWERFUL CONTEMPORARY RELEVANCE

I undertake to refrain from
killing and harming living beings.

I undertake to refrain from
stealing and taking what is not mine.

I undertake to refrain from
causing harm through sexual misconduct.

I undertake to refrain from
false speech, harmful speech, gossip and slander.

I undertake to refrain from
the misuse of intoxicants such as drugs or alcohol
that cause carelessness or loss of awareness.

Many years ago, I wrote these five Buddhist precepts into one of my note-books. Each time I re-read them some fresh insight reveals itself. I find them demanding – to say the least! They hold out a vision of living in harmony with your inner self, with the folk around you and with the wider world. They are an invitation to explore a high degree of self-discipline.

These words may be centuries old, but they hold powerful contemporary relevance. They speak directly to corporate greed, to the superficialities of political spin, to the rape of the environment, to our endless search for 'security', to our fear of 'the other', and to our shared self-indulgence in a world of need.

At first glance, these precepts may seem simple, perhaps unfashionable. Yet as we begin to engage with their implications, it becomes clear that they propel us into creative engagement with the world, that often messy, scandal-ridden place where, amazing as it may seem, God is ever-present. That is why I keep coming back to these words, and why I value the tradition and wisdom in which they are earthed.

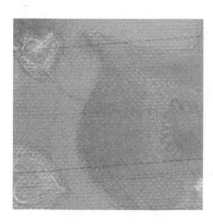

CHRIST'S FRIENDSHIP

In recent times, the churches have spent much time and energy in debating questions of human sexuality. These debates often rend asunder the churches, and leave in their aftermath many wounded women and men. Underlying these discussions are hidden fears, long-held prejudices and the inability to accept difference.

Yet, as I read the gospels, I am always struck by the fact that Jesus met people where they were in life. He saw their potential as people, and valued their rich humanity. And it is in this valuing of the human person that we can move into new depths of understanding, insight and awareness about one another, whatever our differences.

In the following prayer, I try to express something of the movements of my own soul, while at the same time asking God to enlarge my understanding of others. I believe this two-fold path is for us all as we seek Christ's friendship on our journeys.

God of compassion,
you made us
in your own image
and our prayer is
that each day you will
illumine our minds,
enlarge our awareness
and free us from prejudice,
so that we cease to
marginalise,
judge
and condemn others
because of their
sexual orientation.
And, along the way,
help us to
examine with honesty
our own
inner contradictions,
sexual fears
and emotional longings.

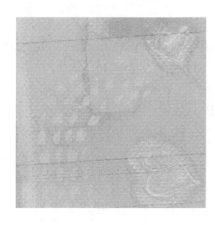

WE ARE HELD IN LOVE

For every step we take towards God, he takes a thousand steps towards us.

PARAPHRASED FROM THE KORAN

Don't you find these words amazingly reassuring? Words of lasting hope as we struggle to make sense of God and of life. It is as if God is rushing towards us in love, welcoming us to the place where our true home exists. These words remind me of the teaching of Jesus, that if only we knock on the door (perhaps even with a hesitant, almost imperceptible knock) God will respond.

Through the years of my ministry, I have met many people whose Christian faith seemed like a great weight to them, something to be endured but never enjoyed. A yoke of burden, never of liberation!

These beautiful words from the Koran speak of a God who sits with us where we sit, in all of our muddle and contradiction. Even the slightest inclination of our hearts toward the divine fills our lives with God.

Saint Simeon, a visionary theologian, put it simply: 'Radiant in his Light, we awaken to the knowledge that we are held in love in every part of our body.'

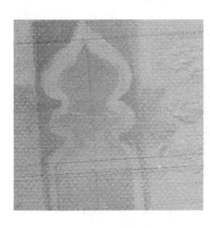

THE GOD OF TIME
AND ETERNITY

This is what you should do:
love the earth and sun and animals,
despise riches,
give alms to everyone who asks,
devote your income and labour to others,
hate tyrants,
argue not concerning God,
have patience and indulgence toward the people,
re-examine all you have been told
in school, or church or any book,
dismiss what insults your very soul,
and your flesh
shall become
a great poem.

WALT WHITMAN,
from the introduction to the 1855 edition of *Leaves of Grass*

Richard Holloway, the former bishop of Edinburgh, quotes these lines from Whitman at the end of his book *Doubts and Loves: What is Left of Christianity*. In this radical book, Richard writes of the essence of Christ's revolutionary and humane teachings and shows why they are of immense contemporary importance. He makes insightful political and cultural connections, offering real spiritual hope to those (including myself) who feel that the church is often fearful of modern, pluralistic society.

Yet why are so many Christians afraid to re-examine any part of their faith in the light of modern society? And why do they react against, and regard as heretics, people who raise these issues?

Years ago, J.B. Phillips, who worked tirelessly to put the Bible into every-day language, reminded his readers that often the God they believed in was too small. Too domesticated. Not the God of earth and heaven, of time and eternity.

Seeking this larger God propels us to re-examine our Christian beliefs, not in order to ditch them, but so that they may be enlarged. Opening our hearts and minds to this kind of intellectual and emotional enquiry does not mean that we uncritically accept every utterance of radical theologians; but are not such writers to be celebrated if they can bring new excitement, enthusiasm and passion to what we think about God, Jesus Christ and the Bible?

Julia McGuiness mirrors something of this search in her poetic magic:

Some people travel in straight lines:
Sat in metal boxes, eyes ahead,
Always mindful of their target,
Moving in obedience to coloured lights and white lines,
Mission accomplished at journey's end.

Some people travel around in circles:
Trudging in drudgery, eyes looking down,
Knowing only too well their daily, unchanging round,
Moving in response to clock and to habit,
Journey never finished yet never begun.

I want to travel in patterns of God's making:
Walking in wonder, gazing all around,
Knowing my destiny, though not my destination,
Moving to the rhythm of the surging of his spirit,
A journey which when life ends, in Christ has just begun.

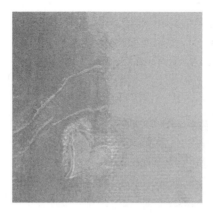

WEAVING OUR FUTURE FROM UNTANGLED THREADS

Speak to me
About the past.
I can discern no meaning in its tapestry.

Help me
Unravel it,
And weave a future
From untangled threads.

FROM A POEM BY MARLENE FINLAYSON,
a member of the Iona Community who lives in Orkney

When I first read Marlene's thought-provoking lines, I sat quietly and meditated on them for a long time. They hold a range of meanings: Our personal pasts. The world's past. God's past. And the mysterious interconnectedness of all of these.

Marlene's lines also bring to mind many questions: In what way does our past and the world's past inform our future? Can we unravel the tangled threads of human history in any meaningful way? And can our awareness of God assist us in this task?

Perhaps one of the ways into an understanding of the past is through silence – by being alive to the deep silences of God in whose hands are held all our pasts and all our futures. The meaning of the past may become more known as we remain still in the Spirit's presence, as we 'rest in God'. The unravelling takes place when our hearts are calm and when, as the Chandogya Upanishad says, 'we are all alone before God'.

Friedrich von Hugel wrote: 'Be silent about great things and let them grow inside you. There is no need for discussion, as that can be limiting and distracting and may make things grow smaller. Before all greatness be silent.'

The past is a mystery, but even a fragmentary understanding of it may bring us a new way in which to look at the future and may be life-restoring and liberating.

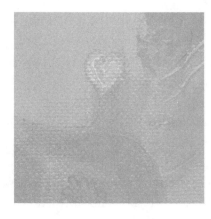

CAN YOU WAIT?

Who brings about peace is called the companion of God in
the work of creation.

TRADITIONAL JEWISH SAYING

> God,
> what an incredible thought!
> This rather limited human being
> with many inner contradictions,
> uncertainties and questions
> is invited
> to be a peacemaker.
>
> Never.

Then the next surprise:
if the invitation is accepted
you call me,
'a companion of God'.
That blows my mind;
it's too much to take in,
especially when today
I just happen to be feeling hassled.

But you are not finished yet.
You also say that
I am a co-creator with you,
the One who made the universe.

All this needs a long time to think about.
Maybe hours,
maybe months,
maybe years.

Maybe a lifetime!

Can you wait?

BLESSED ARE THE PEACEMAKERS

Blessed are the peacemakers for they shall be called God's children.

MATTHEW 5:9

In 2002, Rowan Williams wrote a pamphlet for the Christian Socialist Movement entitled *The Kingdom is Theirs: Five Reflections on the Beatitudes.* In it, he wrote these words:

> Peace costs … Some of the reasons for that cost are to do with us … If we are to make peace, we have to let go of fantasy and obsession and the longing for control. We must be poor in spirit. If we are to make peace, our attitude to the world

around us must not be aggressive and acquisitive. We must be vulnerable and receptive. We have to be meek. If we are to make peace, we must know the need of it. We must let ourselves be hurt by war and violence, oppression and injustice. And we have to learn to mourn. If we are to make peace, we have to feel our own loss and deprivation. In a world of injustice, we must be hungry and thirsty for justice.

No wonder then that those who make peace are to be called God's children. They do God-like things. They are caught up into the making of wholeness on earth.

Prayer

Let us dream. Let us prophesise.
Let us see visions of love, peace and justice.
Let us affirm with humility, with joy, with faith,
*   with courage and in confidence*
that you, O Christ, are the life of the world.

A PRAYER FROM SOUTH AFRICA

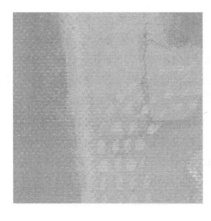

HAND IN HAND

We are in the midst of the world's fastest transformation.
In times of major transformation, two things occur:
A sense of breakdown,
a sense of possibility or breakthrough.

JOAN CHITTISTER,
peace activist and spiritual guide

For many years, Joan, who is a Benedictine sister in the United States, has campaigned tirelessly, both locally and globally, for a more humane social order. Her remarkable witness is rooted in a disciplined life of prayer and in the conviction that listening to scripture and working for lasting justice on the earth go hand in hand. Tragically, given the nature of our times, this is not a conviction acceptable to some Christians, who refuse to see any connection between biblical prophecy and the massive injustices which are such powerful markers of this new century.

In the Old Testament, the prophet Jeremiah looked forward to that day when the exiled people of Israel would return home; when tears would be wiped away and bruised spirits would be made whole again. When from the far corners of the earth would come the blind, broken and obstinate into the outstretched hands of God; when even the hills would shout for joy!

Jeremiah's vision directly relates to our fragile period in history. Today we, too, are 'in exile', and often the work for justice and peace appears unending. The principalities and powers of late-modernity are powerful beyond our understanding. Yet it is also a marker of our age that millions of people are awakening to the truth that this can be a time of breakthrough and of restoration. It is true, as Saint Paul wrote long ago: 'The Spirit comes to help us in our weakness. For we do not know how to pray as we ought, but the Spirit intercedes for us.' (Romans 8:26)

With Joan, I believe that we are at a moment of tremendous possibility in human affairs. And that the restless, surprising, unpredictable energy of God is working in our midst.

The world belongs to God,
THE EARTH AND ALL ITS PEOPLE.

How good it is, how wonderful,
TO LIVE TOGETHER IN UNITY.

Love and faith come together,
JUSTICE AND PEACE JOIN HANDS.

If Christ's disciples keep silent
THESE STONES WOULD SHOUT ALOUD.

Open our lips, O God,
AND OUR MOUTHS SHALL PROCLAIM YOUR PRAISE.

OPENING RESPONSES OF THE MORNING SERVICE, IONA ABBEY

WEAPONS OF GOD

Under certain circumstances fasting is the one weapon which God has given us for use in times of utter helplessness. We do not know its use, or fancy that it begins and ends with mere deprivation of physical food. Absence of food is an indispensable, but not the largest part of it. The largest part is the prayer – communion with God. It more than adequately replaces physical food.

MOHANDAS GANDHI,
in a letter to his colleague Mira Behn, May 8, 1933

Many of the great religious traditions link fasting and prayer. In many churches around the world they are a normal part of Christian discipleship, as I discovered when I was living in India.

Fasting and prayer are 'weapons of God', which have helped many to live more attentively and counter-culturally.

In our own precarious times, how can we rediscover this linkage in a way which is both authentic and life-restoring? Living in a society obsessed with food and consumption, can we, without fanfare, accept that degree of self-surrender?

Gandhi's eloquent letter – written seventy years ago as India struggled for independence – brings to our modern, often comfortable consciousness, a wonderfully powerful and ancient truth.

To recognise evil and not to oppose it
is to surrender your humanity;
to recognise evil and to oppose it
with the weapons of the evil-doer
is to enter into your humanity;
to recognise evil and to oppose it
with the weapons of God
is to enter into your divinity.

MAHATMA GANDHI

Fasting and feasting

Fast from judging others; feast on the Christ dwelling in them.
Fast from emphasis on difference; feast on the unity of life.
Fast from apparent darkness; feast on the reality of life.
Fast from thoughts of illness; feast on the healing power of God.
Fast from words that pollute; feast on phrases that purify.
Fast from discontent; feast on gratitude.
Fast from anger; feast on patience.
Fast from pessimism; feast on optimism.
Fast from worry; feast on divine order.
Fast from complaining; feast on appreciation.
Fast from negatives; feast on affirmatives.
Fast from unrelenting pressures; feast on unceasing prayer.
Fast from hostility; feast on non-resistance.
Fast from bitterness; feast on forgiveness.
Fast from self-concern; feast on compassion for others.
Fast from personal anxiety; feast on eternal truth.
Fast from discouragements; feast on hope.
Fast from facts that depress; feast on verities that uplift.
Fast from lethargy; feast on enthusiasm.
Fast from thoughts that weaken; feast on promises that inspire.
Fast from shadows of sorrow; feast on the sunlight of serenity.
Fast from idle gossip; feast on purposeful silence.

FROM A BENEDICTINE COMMUNITY'S WEBSITE

ANOTHER WAY

One day when I could no longer hear the phrase 'the war on terror' one more time without screaming out loud, I wrote these lines:

Have we forgotten
the wonder of each day
and the magic of each other,
as we speak,
yet again,
these strange words
about
'the war on terror' –
in a world of violence?

Afraid of the stranger,
but perhaps more
fearful of ourselves;
there's weeping in our souls –
in a world of violence.

In these uncertain times
we lock our hearts and doors,
and know we're still on edge –
in a world of violence.

Yet even while imprisoned
in our freedoms,
our hearts still sing of hope –
if given half a chance.

We long to laugh again,
to dream a dream,
to dance in the sun –
in a world of love.

And One still calls
gently in the storm;
for in the midst of fears
there remains
another way,
resonant with life
and tested through the years.

PRESENT CONFUSIONS

The grief of the holy land,
the tortured screams of Iraq,
the bullets and the bombs of Kabul, Sudan, Palestine ...
the rhetoric and spin of Washington and London.

With confused, questioning hearts, God,
we turn again to these words:

'The Word became a human being,
and full of grace and truth lived among us.'

And he, who came on that first Christmas morning,
gently reminds us of another way,
a pilgrim way,
not distant from struggles,
but in their midst;

a way mysteriously calling us
to listen to the cries of the wounded of our world
and to help bear their burdens;
a way which,
amazingly,
renews us with the wonder of love,
rekindling in our hearts
the possibility that we can move forward with hope –
a people of compassion,
committed to sharing.

HOPE

In the introduction to my book *Finding Hope Again: Journeying Through Sorrow and Beyond*, I mentioned the writer Primo Levi and his experience of hope.

Primo Levi was a prisoner in the concentration camp at Auschwitz, and later recorded something of the unspeakable horrors that he had witnessed there. Yet even in this situation of monumental human cruelty, this hell-hole, Levi also witnessed signs of what he calls 'unavoidable hope'. And it was this living hope, this earthed hope, which enabled people to survive another minute, another hour, another day.

Rabbi Jonathan Saks, an Old Testament scholar, recognises this profound hope in the long history of the Jewish people:

'One of the most important distinctions I have learned in the course of reflection on Jewish history is the difference between "optimism" and "hope". Optimism is the belief that things will get better. Hope is the faith that, together, we can make things better. Optimism is a passive virtue, hope an active one. It takes no courage to be an optimist, but it takes a great deal of courage to have hope. Knowing what we do of our past, no Jew can be an optimist. But Jews have never – despite a history of sometimes awesome suffering – given up hope. Not by accident did they call the national anthem of their new state "Hatikvah", meaning "the hope".'

Christians share in this deeply rooted hope, and, like the Jewish people, hear it resonating through the Bible. It is the kind of hope which is 'an active virtue' earthed in the amazingly rich trajectories of our souls. In scripture it is often poetically expressed, as in these words from the prophet Isaiah:

> *The Lord has filled me with his spirit.*
> *He has chosen me and sent me to bring good news to the poor,*
> *to heal the broken-hearted,*
> *to announce release to captives and freedom to those in prison.*
> *To give to those who mourn, joy and gladness instead of grief:*
> *a song of praise instead of sorrow.*

Isaiah 61

THE PARADOXICAL
ORDERING OF OUR LIVES

And David and all the house of Israel were making merry
before the Lord with all their might, with songs and lyres and
harps and tambourines and castanets and cymbals.

2 SAMUEL 6:5

I am playing all the right notes, just not in the right order.

THE COMEDIAN ERIC MORECAMBE

Don't you think Jesus would have responded positively to these words? It's
the story of our lives – or at least it's part of the story of part of our lives! I
don't think these words suggest total confusion – in fact it may be that

they remind us of the rather paradoxical ordering of our lives. And as a person who can live with contradiction, I find them affirming.

Jesus was forever sitting and listening to folk and, like us, a lot of them were playing all the right notes, if not in the right order. I am certain that he recognised this in them and forgave them their mistakes, false starts, dead ends ... their clashes and conflicts. I am certain that he recognised, somewhere in the heart of their confusion, their beauty and potential as people.

Prayer

Jesus, you listen to my prayer
(even though it is far from clear and perfect).
You understand my contradictions and confused longings.
You love and accept me for who I am.

Jesus, reconcile the dissonance in my heart and mind,
make my life a beautiful song to share.

NOT SUCH A BAD PLACE AFTER ALL

When we fail to mourn properly our incomplete lives, then this incompleteness becomes a gnawing restlessness, a bitter centre that robs our lives of delight. Because we do not mourn, we demand that someone or something – a marriage partner, a sexual partner, an ideal family, having children, an achievement, a vocational goal, or a job – take all of our loneliness away. That, of course, is an unreal expectation which invariably leads to bitterness and disappointment. In this life there is no finished symphony. We are built for eternity. Because of that we will, this side of eternity, always be lonely, restless, incomplete.

RONALD ROLHEISER

It took me years to wake up to the basic fact that most of life's symphonies remain unfinished. Many of our hopes and dreams will never come to fruition. Our relationships and friendships will always have painful dimensions of incompleteness.

It is right that we mourn these unfinished symphonies, grieve over them, and try to move on. Yet it is a tough road with many strange, unexpected and threatening twists. At points, the journey can be overwhelming.

Yet in learning to mourn our unfinished symphonies we make a variety of discoveries; and one of them is that we may not be in such a bad place after all! Becoming aware of all the incomplete parts of our lives can help us to move into a more gentle estimation of ourselves. As the old slogan says: 'Let go, let God.'

I remember a friend telling me that life is all about 'releasing our baggage every day' – in other words, learning to live with incompleteness. And in connection with that challenge, I like this prayer, which comes from Australia.

God, give me the strength to hold on, and the strength to let go.

MICHAEL LEUNIG

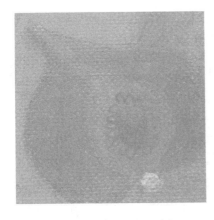

NO WONDER PEOPLE FOLLOWED HIM

He (Bob Geldof) is a lot like Saint Vincent de Paul who could have had a good career in the church but chose to do Christ's work instead.

WORDS OF CLIVE JAMES,
social commentator and broadcaster

I think if we don't see the gloriously funny side of these words, we are spiritually impoverished! Many years ago, the distinguished Scottish theologian Elizabeth Templeton wrote: 'I am sure that God is alive and well in this country, but mercifully not dependent on the churches alone for his effective disclosure.'

One of things that has always attracted me to the person and ministry of Jesus is that he really seemed to enjoy being with people who were, in one way or another, on the edges of institutional religion. Certainly he was grounded in his own faith traditions, but he kept reaching beyond them, and reconfiguring them. He intuitively recognised where the authentic spirit of God was alive – and knew that its location was often far outwith the temple structures of his day. No wonder people followed him!

Almost one hundred years ago, Albert Schweitzer, in his book *The Quest of the Historical Jesus*, wrote:

'He comes to us as one unknown, without a name, as of old, by the lake-side, he came to those men who did not know who he was. He says the same words, "Follow me!", and sets us to those tasks which he must fulfil in our time. He commands. And to those who hearken to him, whether wise or unwise, he will reveal himself in the peace, the labours, the conflicts and the suffering that they may experience in his fellowship, and as an ineffable mystery they will learn who he is.'

GOD WHO JOURNEYS WITH US

We believe in God
who takes our smallest moment of hope
and grows it forth like a tree
with spreading branches
for the sheltering of new life.

We believe in Jesus Christ
who walks tall among us,
seen in our faces, felt in our hearts,
bedded deep in the longing of our souls
for all that is true, just and full of hope.

We believe in the Holy Spirit
who waits on our moments of openness

and springs into the unknowns
with joy and delight,
that we might be called on
beyond where we thought we could go
where every step is walked on holy ground.

DOROTHY McRAE-McMAHON,
Australian writer and theologian

I often return to these wonderful words, which are words of wisdom for these rather strange times in which we all find ourselves. At their core, they are words of profound hope.

In clear, everyday language, these words carry us to the basic truth that our lives, however hard and uncertain, are ultimately grounded in a sacred mystery – the amazing grace of a God who journeys with us.

I would like to suggest that you read this creed again as a whole, and afterwards choose a line, or a couple of lines, to reflect upon over a few days or weeks. Sit quietly with a line and allow the words and thoughts to penetrate your soul, to become a part of your spiritual search; try to find a Bible passage or verse which reflects its wisdom. Allow yourself to be surprised by the Spirit 'who waits on our moments of openness and springs into the unknowns with joy and delight'.

I am sure that, as the words empower you and affirm your own pilgrimage in God, you will, like me, return to them many times.

PERHAPS IF WE
REALLY BELIEVED

I will not die an unlived life.
I will not go in fear
Of falling or catching fire.
I choose to inhabit my days,
To allow my living to open to me,
To make me less afraid,
More accessible,
To loosen my heart
Until it becomes a wing,
A torch, a promise.
I choose to risk my significance:
To live.
So that which came to me as seed,
Goes to the next as blossom;
And that which came to me as blossom,
Goes on as fruit.

Dawna Markova

Every time I read this poem, it touches my soul. I have shared it with different people in many countries, and, like me, they have been moved, often to tears, by its words, which hold the promise of new possibilities in God. My daughter-in-law, Ange, read it at Dorothy's funeral.

A few weeks before her death, Dorothy wrote a powerful reflection on these words, for she believed that they were of particular significance to those of us working for peace and justice in such precarious times.

Underlying Dawna Markova's beautiful poem is the conviction that our lives can become richly productive of authentic love, no matter where we are, and even in situations where we feel powerless. This productivity – which relates to the invitation that Christ was constantly giving to those he met – is directly linked both to our inner strength and to our inner vulnerability. The 'loosening of our heart' is a life-long spiritual task. And the fact that a liberated heart can become a wing, a torch, a promise to help others on the journey of life is something truly miraculous.

Perhaps if we really believed that our one, small life on this earth could be productive of such spiritual truth and treasure, we would celebrate each day with more awareness and greater joy.

As an old Eastern Orthodox prayer says: 'Set our hearts on fire with love to thee, O Christ, that in that flame we may love thee and our neighbour as ourselves.'

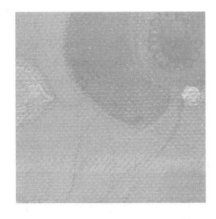

A JOURNEY IN
UNDERSTANDING

Susan was teaching school in Oxford but she felt she would like to come to India to help in some work here. She arrived in Madras and we suggested that Susan be involved with a school which has links to our church. It was agreed that she should work as a kind of house-mother and also do some teaching. In this particular school many of the children are from very poor families. Often these families live in small rooms in a slum area or on the pavement.

In her first few weeks at this school, Susan found so many things lacking. There was little equipment, few books and hardly anything in the way of material comfort; it all seemed so incredibly different from her modern comprehensive in Oxford. In fact, it seemed like a million miles away, not just six thousand. She had entered another world – not just a different world – and she hardly knew how to begin to help. It was overwhelming, especially when she began to learn something of the daily battles involved in living on 150 rupees per month.

Yet, as the weeks went by, Susan began to see the situation differently. Her journey of understanding (experienced by so many volunteers when they come to India) had begun. Or to put it in the words of the writer Antoine de Saint-Exupéry: 'And now here is my secret: it is only with the heart that one can see rightly; what is essential is invisible to the eye.'

Certainly the kids were poor, terribly poor by British standards, but they were gentle and caring of one another. Yes, there was little equipment, but the hostel in which the children stayed seemed to be a place of love. And, amazingly, despite the lack of material comforts, the children were happy and full of life – often radiantly happy. Of course there were problems and many hidden sorrows and hardships, but the positive things often outweighed the difficulties. There was a deep sense of solidarity as people, together, faced the various struggles.

And in this 'poor' and 'deprived' situation, which was so completely different from anything she had experienced, Susan began to feel very happy and to discover new dimensions of her personality. She was greatly touched by the concern which the children and the staff had for her. Here she was accepted as a member of the family. And in that atmosphere of caring, Susan began to change as a person. Her values and attitudes changed. She no longer saw the school as a poor place, but as a place where she belonged as a person and where she was welcomed for who she was. She had come to 'help' but she soon discovered it was she who was being helped, although she gave so much.

Last Sunday, Susan left Madras and returned home on the Madras-Bombay-London flight. It was a tearful farewell, and one day Susan hopes to return to this place where she has found so much joy. In these few short months here she has been given new eyes to see and countless new insights about our essential togetherness as human beings on this small planet.

As we recall these experiences of Susan here in Madras, we don't believe for a moment that it is only by travelling six thousand miles to another culture that we can be participants in this journey of understanding. That transformation in our attitude can begin right where we are – anywhere in the world. It starts by being open, within our hearts and minds, to God's possibilities; or as Brother Roger of Taizé says: 'Let the risen Christ sing in you the radiant gift of life, to the point that the springs of jubilation never run dry.'

This journey of understanding is essential if our human family is to survive. And as a way of living it stands in direct contradiction to the many inhuman and depersonalising policies of governments, both here in India and in other places. We have lost so many of our human connections and in doing so we have become prisoners of ourselves. Our world is full of barriers – and along with these barriers comes an incredible amount of fear.

The kind of experience which Susan had in South India is a small but significant step in reminding us that fear and its concomitants can be replaced when we begin to see through the eyes of the other person, the eyes of our brother or sister. When we begin to understand that, we stand – despite all of our external differences – in solidarity with each other.

DOROTHY AND PETER MILLAR
(from *Letters from Madras*, 1988)

WE ARE NEVER ALONE

OR ABANDONED

In work and worship
GOD IS WITH US
Gathered and scattered
GOD IS WITH US
Now and always
GOD IS WITH US. AMEN

FROM THE DAILY OFFICE OF THE IONA COMMUNITY

It would be true to say that thousands of people have used this prayer, not just in Iona Abbey, but in countless places around the world. It forms the closing responses of the Act of Prayer of the Iona Community and is prayed by many on a daily basis.

Perhaps what I value most about this prayer is its simplicity, yet breadth of vision. Gentle yet directive, inspiring and challenging, it wonderfully encompasses the material and the spiritual, the local and the global, the realities of time and of eternity – and not too many prayers do all of that in six short lines!

Even when one is in a dark tunnel, this prayer announces fresh hope. We are never alone or abandoned in this often uncertain world. God is always present. God within us, beside us, before us. God permeating our daily lives.

Or in the rich words of Saint Paul:

> *May Christ make his home in your hearts through faith:*
> *May your roots and foundations be in his love.*
> *May you, with all God's people, have the power to understand*
> *the breadth and length and height and depth of Christ's love.*

EPHESIANS 3:17–19

JOURNEY BLESSING

May our journey ahead
Be blessed
With God's
Laughter,
Silences,
Risks,
Challenges,
Healings,
Questions,
Promises,
Protests,
Answers,
Tears,
Solidarity,
Often uncomfortable peace,
And
Compassion-filled surprises,
Perhaps
All
In
One
Day.

PETER MILLAR

SOURCES AND ACKNOWLEDGEMENTS

Every effort has been made to trace copyright holders of all items reproduced in this book. We would be glad to hear from anyone whom we have been unable to contact so that any omissions can be rectified in future editions.

Page 13: 'To become aware of the sacramental nature of the cosmos' by Ron Ferguson, from *Chasing the Wild Goose: The Story of the Iona Community*, Wild Goose Publications, 1998, ISBN 1901557006.

Page 14: 'Apprehend God in all things', Meister Eckhart, from *The Iona Abbey Worship Book*, Wild Goose Publications, 2001, ISBN 1901557502.

Page 17: 'We will have to repent in this generation …', Martin Luther King, from 'Letter from Birmingham Jail', April 16, 1963.

Page 21: 'A community of pilgrims needs to abandon clutter', taken from *The Eye of the Storm*, published and copyright 1997 by Darton, Longman and Todd Ltd, and used by permission of the publishers.

Page 23: 'I am proud' by Oodgeroo of the tribe Noonuccal, from *My People*, 3e, The Jacaranda Press, 1990. Reproduced by permission of John Wiley & Sons Australia.

Page 32: 'It's the hug' by Peter Millar, from *Finding Hope Again: Journeying Through Sorrow & Beyond*, Peter Millar, Canterbury Press 2003, ISBN 1853114383. Used by permission of SCM/Canterbury Press.

Page 35: 'Be patient toward all that is unresolved in your heart', from *Letters To A Young Poet* by Rainer Maria Rilke, translated by M.D. Herter Norton. Copyright 1934, 1954 by W.W. Norton & Company, Inc., renewed © 1962, 1982 by M.D. Herter Norton. Used by permission of W.W. Norton & Company, Inc.

Page 63: Davie McCuish quote, from Fergal Keane's *Forgotten Britain*. Used by permission of Davie McCuish and Fergal Keane.

Page 71: The 'developed' world, from *Letters from Madras*, © Dorothy and Peter Millar, 1988.

Page 72: 'O God, strengthen us in our desire', from a prayer by Philip Newell, *The Iona Abbey Worship Book*, Wild Goose Publications 2001, ISBN 1901557502.

Page 78: 'Jesus, teach us to accept each other as you accept us …' adapted from a prayer by Ian Fraser from *Strange Fire: Life Stories and Prayers*, Wild Goose Publications, 1994, ISBN 094798867X.

Page 79: 'Shanti's journey', from *Letters from Madras*, © Dorothy and Peter Millar,1988.

Page 81: Prayer of St Francis, from *The Iona Abbey Worship Book*, Wild Goose Publications 2001, ISBN 1901557502.

Page 83: 'Great Spirit, give us hearts to understand', as found in the United Nations Environment Programme Environmental Sabbath kit of April 1988.

Page 89: 'We look up and see the stars shining above', by Eddie Kneebone, used by permission of the author.

Page 94: 'More than 11 million children in sub-Saharan Africa have now lost one or both parents to Aids', from the article '11m lose parents to Aids' by Sarah Boseley, *The Guardian* newspaper, Thursday, November 27, 2003. Used by permission of *The Guardian*.

Page 96: Conversation in the reading 'Christ of Gethsemane' taken from the article 'Rebels who have lost their cause', by Robert Lacville, *The Guardian*, December 2, 1999. Used by permission of Robert Lacville.

Page 120: 'Peace costs' by Rowan Williams, from *The Kingdom is Theirs: Five Reflections on the Beatitudes*, Rowan Williams, Christian Socialist Movement, 2002. Used by permission of the Christian Socialist Movement.

Page 122: 'We are in the midst of the world's fastest transformation', Joan Chittister, OSB. Used by permission of Benetvision, on behalf of Joan Chittister.

Page 123: Opening responses from the morning service © Iona Community, from *The Iona Abbey Worship Book*, Wild Goose Publications 2001, ISBN 1901557502.

Page 127: 'Fasting and feasting' can be found on many websites. Original source unknown.

Page 133: 'One of the most important distinctions I have learned in the course of reflection on Jewish history' by Rabbi Jonathan Saks, from *The Dignity of Difference: How to Avoid the Clash of Civilizations*, Rabbi Jonathan Saks. Used by permission of Louise Greenberg Books Ltd.

Page 134: Eric Morecambe quote used by permission of Billy Marsh Associates Ltd.

Page 136: 'When we fail to mourn properly our incomplete lives', by Ronald Rolheiser, from *Finding Spirituality*, Hodder and Stoughton. Reproduced by permission of Hodder and Stoughton Limited. Also used by the permission of Random House/Doubleday US.

Page 137: 'God, give me the strength to hold on' by Michael Leunig. Used by permission of Michael Leunig.

Page 138: Clive James quote used by permission of Norman North, on behalf of Clive James.

Elizabeth Templeton quote used by permission of Elizabeth Templeton.

THE IONA COMMUNITY

The Iona Community, founded in 1938 by the Revd George MacLeod, then a parish minister in Glasgow, is an ecumenical Christian community committed to seeking new ways of living the Gospel in today's world. Initially working to restore part of the medieval abbey on Iona, the Community today remains committed to 'rebuilding the common life' through working for social and political change, striving for the renewal of the church with an ecumenical emphasis, and exploring new, more inclusive approaches to worship, all based on an integrated understanding of spirituality.

The Community now has over 240 Members, about 1500 Associate Members and around 1500 Friends. The Members – women and men from many denominations and backgrounds (lay and ordained), living throughout Britain with a few overseas – are committed to a fivefold Rule of devotional discipline, sharing and accounting for use of time and money, regular meeting, and action for justice and peace.

At the Community's three residential centres – the Abbey and the MacLeod Centre on Iona, and Camas Adventure Camp on the Ross of Mull – guests are welcomed from March to October and over Christmas. Hospitality is provided for over 110 people, along with a unique opportunity, usually through week-long programmes, to extend horizons and forge relationships through sharing an experience of the common life in worship, work, discussion and relaxation. The Community's shop on Iona, just outside the Abbey grounds, carries an attractive range of books and craft goods.

The Community's administrative headquarters are in Glasgow, which also serves as a base for its work with young people, the Wild Goose Resource Group working in the field of worship, a bi-monthly magazine, *Coracle*, and a publishing house, Wild Goose Publications.

For information on the Iona Community contact:
The Iona Community, Fourth Floor, Savoy House, 140 Sauchiehall Street, Glasgow G2 3DH,
UK. Phone: 0141 332 6343
e-mail: ionacomm@gla.iona.org.uk; web: www.iona.org.uk

For enquiries about visiting Iona, please contact:
Iona Abbey, Isle of Iona, Argyll PA76 6SN, UK. Phone: 01681 700404
e-mail: ionacomm@iona.org.uk